W9-BEU-877

SPALDING.

Steve Alford & Ed Schilling

MASTERS PRESS

A Division of Howard W. Sams & Company

Published by Masters Press (A Division of Howard W. Sams & Co.)
2647 Waterfront Pkwy. E. Drive, Suite 300
Indianapolis, IN 46214

© 1995 Steve Alford and Ed Schilling
All rights reserved

Published 1995
Printed in the United States of America

No part of this publication may be reproduced, stored in a retrievl system, or transmit-
ted, in any form or by any means, electronic, mechanical, photocopying, recording, or
otherwise, without the prior permission of Masters Press.

10 9 8 7 6 5 4 3 2

Library of Congress Cataloging-in-Publication Data

Alford, Steve.
  Basketball guard play / Steve Alford & Ed Schilling.
       p.   cm.
   ISBN 1-57028-024-X (pbk.)
   1. Basketball --Offense. 2. Basketball -- Psychological aspects.
I. Schilling, Ed, 1966- . II. Title.

GV889.A54   1995   95-19947
796.332'2--dc20   CIP

TABLE OF CONTENTS

Credits:

Edited by Mark Montieth

Cover design by Suzanne Lincoln

Front cover photos © Brian Spurlock

Back cover photo of Ed Schilling courtesy of the Pharos-Tribune, Logansport, IN

Back cover photo of Steve Alford © Chuck Savage

Interior photos by Richard Voorhees, except for photos on pages 4, 19, and 64 provided by Indiana University Sports Information Department and photos on pages 3, 6, 9, and 40 provided by Ed Schilling.

Special thanks to Pat Brady and Phil Velikan for editorial assistance.

FOREWORD

▪ ▪

All fathers enjoy talking about their sons, and I'm certainly no different. I've seen Steve earn a Mr. Basketball title in high school, play on a gold medal-winning team in the Olympic Games, captain an NCAA championship team and play four years in the NBA.

As a father I have great passion for my son, but as a head coach for 29 years I believe I can view his basketball career with some objectivity. Steve was a "gym rat" from the beginning, and basketball shaped his development as a child. In fact, he learned to count by keeping track of the score during my games when he was three years old.

In 1969 Steve packed his first gym bag and played in a first- and second-grade YMCA league. He was only in kindergarten at the time, but already was getting an opportunity to play with older players. He scored one point in his first game—a humble beginning to be sure, but a beginning just the same.

I later took the head coaching job at Martinsville High School, the home of the legendary former UCLA coach, Johnny Wooden. It was during my four years in Martinsville that Steve began to blossom. One of my players, Jerry Sichting, later of the Indiana Pacers and Boston Celtics, became his idol. Steve tried to duplicate everything Jerry did. I was appreciative that Steve had someone of Jerry's ability and moral fiber to follow.

During Steve's fourth grade year at Poston Road Elementary School, he won the Indiana Elk's Hoop Shoot contest. He hit 24 of 25 free throws to win the district competition and advance to the nationals in Kansas City. He didn't fare as well there, however, and took the defeat hard. While the other kids enjoyed the post-shooting festivities, Steve cried over his defeat. It was then that I realized the depths of Steve's competitive spirit.

In 1975 I interviewed for a job at New Castle Chrysler High School, home of the world's largest high school gymnasium: 9,350 seats. As soon as Steve and his younger brother Sean laid eyes on the place, it was all over. This was to be their high school home. During Steve's senior season, many games had the "Sold Out" sign in the ticket window.

As Steve's playing career progressed through elementary school and junior high school, his burning desire to excel began to show more and more. Upon entering high school, however, he suddenly dropped to low man on the totem pole as a freshman on the varsity team.

Steve made a major decision after that season. Rather than grow discouraged and give up, he rededicated himself to basketball. We designed an individual workout program to begin refining his skills. He began to mature physically. As a result he had a great high school career, scoring more than 2,100 points, with a high game of 57.

Steve reaped many individual honors. Not only was he named Mr. Basketball for the state of Indiana in 1983, but he also was named the Fellowship of Christian Athletes' national Player of the Year. He also decided to attend Indiana University, where he played on the NCAA championship team in 1987.

Steve maintained other interests besides basketball while in college. He was president of the local chapter of the Fellowship of Christian Athletes, for example. I believe Steve developed a clear understanding of what hard work and dedication can bring, not only to an athlete but to all walks of life.

Steve's NBA career ended after four seasons that brought a great deal of frustration, but he is truly happier in his new life as a coach. The roles of father, husband and coach are much more fitting for him. He has enjoyed much success and happiness in each of those roles, and he is reaping the benefits of the discipline and work ethic he learned from his playing career.

Steve faces many new and different challenges in his job as head coach at Southwest Missouri State University. One of them will be dealing with me; I'll be one of his assistant coaches. But I know he can succeed. The same qualities that helped make him a successful player will continue to contibute to his coaching success.

Hopefully those who read this book can learn some of the lessons Steve has learned — not just for basketball, but for life.

Sam Alford

FOREWORD

■■■

Ed Schilling, Jr. started with a distinct size disadvantage as he began his long road to basketball success. Although I am 6-foot-5, his mother is 5-2. He apparently got his height from his mother's side of the family. Despite being short and slender as a young boy, Ed dedicated himself to becoming a successful basketball player.

Perhaps his keen interest in the game came from tagging along with me as I played in amateur basketball tournaments all over the Midwest. At the age of three he would pack his athletic bag and go on road trips with our team. He warmed up with us, sat on the bench and joined us in the locker room.

Later, he began doing endless drills and taking advantage of every opportunity to improve his skills. As an indication of his dedication, he dribbled his basketball to Indianapolis Public School #84 each day. One day he lost control of the ball and it was run over by a car. Perhaps realizing the consequences of careless ballhandling helped him establish assist records at Lebanon High School and at Miami University of Ohio.

Ed's tremendous dedication to his goal not only kept him out of trouble, but laid a foundation that has helped him throughout his adult life. He became the youngest high school head basketball coach in the country at age 22. He was the youngest to coach in the McDonald's Capitol Classic All-Star game at 25. Now 29, he recently completed a four-year career at Logansport High School, where he was the youngest head coach in one of the nation's toughest conferences, the North Central Conference. Next season he'll begin a new career as an assistant at the University of Massachusetts.

Ed's drive also enabled him to become an honor student at Miami. He was awarded the school's highest academic honor, the Mortar Board. He is a director of the nationally renowned Five-Star Basketball Camp. He has been a featured speaker at various state teaching conferences. He is active in his church, influencing many athletic and non-athletic students toward a morally appropriate life.

As his father, I am most humble in my respect and admiration of this young man. He is a positive addition to his community, a positive role model for young people, a dedicated and conscientious husband and father, and a loyal member of his extended family.

Ed Schilling, Jr. eventually grew to become a strong, 6-2 highly successful athlete. The growth about which I am most proud, however, is his development as a person.

Ed Schilling, Sr.

INTRODUCTION

It has been said that a coach with poor big men but good guards can win, but a coach with good big men but poor guards will be fired. This might be a slight exaggeration, but it is true to a large extent. Most possessions in basketball, offensively and defensively, begin with guard play. As former Division I college guards and current coaches, we want to help you improve your guard play.

The guards control the tempo and flow of nearly every game. The guards are the front line of the defense. The guards handle the ball and initiate the offense. The guards create opportunities for the post players by getting them the ball in the right place at the right time and by hitting perimeter shots to draw defensive pressure away from the inside.

The guards often determine the outcome of close games by hitting or missing crucial free throws or field goals, by how they handle the ball against defensive pressure or by getting the ball to an open teammate. Most game-winning plays involve a guard in a substantial way.

Guards must be the most fundamental, versatile and skilled players on a team. Tall players are rare, and have a built-in advantage. But plenty of smaller players are available to play guard. Those who make the team and excel are the ones who have developed their skills, their toughness and their poise.

ED: *As a high school freshman I stood 5-foot-7 and weighed about 125 pounds. But I had a dream of playing college basketball.*

I was barely more than 6-0 and weighed 160 pounds by my senior year in high school. But I was part of a high school team that compiled a 63-13 record despite having no player taller than 6-2. I averaged just 9.2 points per game, but still was chosen to play in a major high school All-America game called the Thoroughbred Classic before 10,000 fans. Obviously, I did some things well besides score — like run the team and record nearly as many assists as points.

Ed tries to convince Steve he really did need to play defense.

I signed a scholarship with Miami University in Oxford, Ohio. There I was fortunate to set all of the school's assist records, and I still hold the single-game assist record in the Mid-American Conference with 17.

However, seven games into my sophomore season I suffered a severe knee injury, tearing my anterior cruciate ligament and both cartilages in my right knee. Although I worked hard to rehabilitate the knee and was able to play fairly well after that, I never got back to my previous level of play.

I share this background to make the point that guards can accomplish a great deal despite limitations in size and scoring ability. Dedication and the proper development of the fundamentals can make dreams become a reality — my career was proof of that.

STEVE: *I grew up in a basketball environment that taught me to have a strong work ethic, a tough mental approach, and, most importantly, a love for the game.*

I faced many doubters of my dreams. As a freshman in high school I stood 5-10 and weighed 125 pounds. Many people thought I was simply too small to have much success with basketball, and their doubts were confirmed when I averaged just one point and shot 69% from the foul line my freshman season with the high school varsity team.

By my senior year I stood 6-1 and tipped the scales at 155. I was able to lead my high school team to the final eight of the state tournament while averaging 37 points a game and shooting 94 percent from the foul line. Later that spring I was voted Mr. Basketball in the state of Indiana. I was also able to compete in the National Sports Festival and win a gold medal.

I received a scholarship to Indiana University, where I renewed my acquaintance with the doubters, who did not believe I was big enough or tough enough to play in the Big Ten. I cracked the starting lineup in my second game and never looked back. I averaged 16 points a game, led the nation by hitting 92 percent of my foul shots, and was named the Big Ten's Freshman of the Year. We reached the final eight of the NCAA tournament that season by defeating No. 1-ranked North Carolina - a team that included players named Michael Jordan and Sam Perkins. Later that summer I was chosen to play for the U.S. Olympic Team that won the gold medal.

I was Indiana's team MVP all four seasons of my career and scored more than 2,400 points, a Big Ten record at the time. I was voted the 1987 Big Ten Player of the Year, we captured the 1987 NCAA championship and I was chosen an All-American. I was the 26th player chosen in the NBA draft that year, and played four years with the Dallas Mavericks and Golden State Warriors.

I introduce myself to you in this manner only to make the point that size and weight are only one aspect of basketball. My dreams came true because I understood the importance of hard work and discipline. Hopefully this book will help inspire you to set high standards for yourself and pursue your dreams.

THE MENTAL GAME

Some coaches believe the mental side of basketball is more important than the physical aspect. Others believe that the physical aspect is more important. Either way, talent alone won't enable you to achieve your goals. You must develop your mental game as well.

Look at the players at any level of competition and you'll notice that the truly great ones have more going for them than raw talent. They are generally mature, disciplined, well-behaved people off the court as well as on the court. They have achieved a high level of performance in the mental aspect as well as the physical aspect.

The mental aspect of basketball includes five elements: leadership, toughness, attitude, discipline and confidence. Those who have learned these traits are sure to be better players, regardless of their physical limitations.

LEADERSHIP

Leaders are special people, because there aren't many of them. But unlike great athletes, leaders are made, not born. Anybody can learn the characteristics of a good leader if he makes the effort. A team without effective leadership is like a car without a steering wheel. It will travel without direction and will not reach its intended destination. In the case of a basketball team, this means it won't win as many games, or championships, as it could.

Coaches cannot provide all the leadership a team needs. The players must assume this responsibility as well, and guards happen to be in the best position to do so. This doesn't mean other players cannot be great leaders; they can. But guards, by the nature of their position, have the best opportunity to be leaders. And remember, leadership is an opportunity, not a burden.

Guards have the ball more than other players and they can see what is happening on the court better than other players. Therefore, they are in the best position to be an extension of the coaching staff and a go-between for the other players. Look at most teams, particularly at younger levels, and you'll see that the captains are usually guards. This isn't just a coincidence.

On the court, leadership can be displayed in many ways: getting the ball to the right person at the right time, accepting the responsibility to take an important shot, not taking bad shots, playing hard ... in general, setting an example for winning basketball.

More than anything, leadership means accepting responsibility and showing poise. Sometimes that even means taking responsibility for something that isn't your fault.

For example, as a guard you might throw a pass that should be caught but gets fumbled away. Instead of criticizing that player, take the blame for the pass. He or she will know whose fault it was but will be inspired to work a little harder — perhaps get the next rebound, or work harder on defense — to make up for the mistake.

The leader also sets an example by not complaining. If the team leader is constantly complaining to the referees, the teammates play off of that and are more likely to do the same. Even if a call is bad — and bad calls will be made — a leader doesn't make a scene. He or she talks to the referee calmly and then forgets it.

A leader takes the same approach with teammates during a game or practice by encouraging them when they are struggling, or telling them when they aren't playing hard enough. Criticism should always be constructive, however. Saying, "Come on, you're too good to play like this!" is far better than scowling and saying, "What's wrong with you today?"

■■

STEVE: *I had the opportunity to play with Michael Jordan on the 1984 U.S. Olympic team. I don't think I've ever played with or against a better leader. He had more athletic ability than anybody on the team, but he was always a good leader. He played hard in practice all the time; even during tedious drills he showed a good attitude toward his coaches and teammates, and he had fun.*

This was a guy who knew he was going to be able to turn professional and make a lot of money. If anybody could have justified taking it easy in practice it was him — but he didn't, and that set an example for the rest of the players. I was a young college player at the time and not the leader of my team yet. I learned a great deal from him that summer.

■■

Leadership can't be turned on and off like a water faucet. The games are only the tip of the iceberg. Leadership is equally important in practice, in the classroom and whenever the team is together. If you don't show consistent leadership, the players won't respect you enough to follow your lead when it counts the most: during games. If you're late to class, show a poor attitude toward your teachers, get poor grades or get into trouble outside of school, you undermine your leadership with the team.

One of the best times to show leadership is at the end of a difficult practice, when everyone else is exhausted and complaining. A player who shrugs it off and maintains

Ed helps up the late Len Bias during an N.C.A.A. tournament game held at the University of Dayton Arena in Dayton, Ohio.

a cheerful attitude by treating it like an enjoyable, productive practice can lift the entire team's spirit.

A leader also performs well in the classroom, taking care of the little things such as being on time, being prepared and participating in classroom activities. Be a risk-taker in class discussions and help get people involved. It takes some courage, but people ultimately will respect you for it.

This is important for the obvious reasons, but it also has practical benefits. A high school player can't get a college scholarship without succeeding in the classroom, and a college player can't maintain eligibility without making passing grades. The same discipline that leads to success on the basketball court will pay off away from the court, too.

Keep it positive

One of the primary responsibilities of a leader is to help make sure the atmosphere is positive whenever the players are together. One of the most important things to watch for is the amount of teasing or "cracking" on players that goes on. It is common for players to get on each other over little things, like tastes in clothing or music, and there's nothing wrong with this within certain limits.

Too often, however, this seemingly harmless game goes too far and players become angry and resentful toward one another. Some people are more sensitive than others and don't like to be kidded. A leader realizes this and makes sure nobody's feelings are being hurt.

You would be surprised how sensitive some players can be, even at the college or professional level. This is just human nature. A leader needs to be willing to step forward and say, "All right, that's enough," or direct the conversation to something else. If you know what makes a player angry or upset, make it a point to keep the conversation away from that area.

A lot of players, particularly young ones, are insecure and enjoy teasing someone else as a way of making themselves feel better. And it's always easy to gang up on one guy. If Joe makes a funny insult about Michael, pretty soon everybody joins in and takes a shot at Michael.

Say Michael hasn't been shooting well lately and Joe says, "Man, Mike, think you'll hit a shot anytime this decade?" Pretty soon other teammates are making fun of Michael's shooting. If this happens, what are the chances Michael will shoot well in the next game? What if Michael has a chance to hit a game-winning free throw, but he's thinking about the jokes his teammates had made in the locker room when he steps to the line? Will he hit it? Probably not.

A good leader will turn it around. If Joe says something to pump up Michael, even in a lighthearted way, other players are likely to join in. If so, Michael is much more likely to hit a crucial shot, because he'll have more confidence. Positive things snowball as rapidly as negative things. A leader tosses positive snowballs.

ED: *I remember my second game my freshman year at Miami. We were playing at Purdue, which was a big game for us. Purdue had just beaten Kentucky, which was ranked in the top five at the time, and Purdue was ranked, too. I was nervous about it because I knew the team members from my old high school would be there watching.*

The night before the game I roomed with Ron Harper, who was our best player and went on to become a great player in the NBA. We stayed up that night watching the highlights on ESPN. I remember they showed David Rivers from Notre Dame, and Ron said, "Yeah, he's good, but I'd rather have you out there." He talked to me about how much confidence he had in me and how I was getting the ball to the right people at the right time. It really lifted me up.

I ended up playing 39 minutes and I had nine assists and one turnover. A lot of that was because of the leadership Ron Harper showed in the hotel room the night before the game. And yes, we won the game.

Never underestimate the power of words. Some people, whether they're athletes or not, grow up hearing negative comments from people. "You'll never amount to anything." "Why can't you do anything right?" "You're a loser." Things like that have a huge impact on people. A lot of people in prison are there because they've heard those kinds of remarks throughout their lives. All they've done is lived up — or down, really — to what others have expected of them.

Good leadership helps create an environment that leads to success — one where nobody wants star treatment, everybody is confident in his teammates, and, most of all, confident in himself. This carries over to a cohesive team that plays together and performs well at crucial moments in games.

STEVE: *This was never more evident than my senior year at Indiana when four of our starters hit last-second game-winning shots. I hit a shot at Michigan to win a game. Dean Garrett hit a shot to end a triple-overtime game at Wisconsin. Ricky Calloway hit a shot to beat LSU in the NCAA tournament. And Keith Smart hit the biggest shot of all to beat Syracuse for the national championship.*

The other starter, Daryl Thomas, had originally taken the shot against LSU, but missed the rim and Calloway rebounded it. Thomas might have failed on his shot, but at least he was willing to take it. If he had tried to pass off, we might not have gotten off a shot in time. Thomas also had the poise to pass up what would have been a bad shot against

Syracuse in the national championship game and get the ball to Smart, who hit a more simple baseline jumper.

His poise was partially the result of good leadership. We had established the attitude that any of us could hit a big shot. Nobody had an ego problem or was insecure. We just played for the best shot possible, and when you do that things will work out most of the time.

Against Syracuse, if we had said, "OK let's get the ball to Steve," we probably wouldn't have scored and wouldn't have won the national championship. Everybody probably was expecting me to shoot, but we didn't care who got the glory. Smart was a junior college transfer who was in his first year on the team, but he felt comfortable enough to take the shot — and make it.

■■

Communicate!

Good leaders communicate with their teammates and coaches, and have the courage to stand up for what's right. Many internal problems can be avoided if a leader recognizes them and heads them off by bringing them into the open.

Don't ever underestimate the importance of this. Many teams with great talent do not win as many games as they can because of internal conflicts, such as jealousy over who is getting to shoot the most and resentment over the way they are being treated. Leadership has a domino effect. One good display of it can inspire other examples, and it becomes contagious. Bad leadership, on the other hand, is like a cancer that spreads and infects an entire team.

A small negative in October or November, such as a petty jealousy or argument, can become a major problem by March and keep a team from achieving its potential if it is not resolved. Players can recognize such things more easily than coaches, and the leadership must come forward to keep potential problems in check.

Leaders don't have to be the stars of the team, either. Anybody can work hard in practice, show a good attitude, and encourage his teammates. In fact, some of the most effective leaders are older players who don't play much but keep a good attitude. This is particularly true in the NBA, where a veteran player in the last year or two of his career can have a tremendous influence on a team's morale and attitude. It also can be true in high school, however. Imagine how much respect a senior who doesn't start will get if he or she shows a positive attitude.

So many things can be done to exhibit leadership. Be the first one off the bench to greet the other players as they come off the court for a time-out. Find something to say to a teammate that will lift his or her spirits. Stick up for a teammate who is being treated unfairly. Small acts like those can have more impact on a player than anything the coach can do.

■■■

ED: *When I was in college I made it a habit to stop by my teammates' dorm rooms from time to time and ask about anything that might be bothering them. For example, did they think one player was shooting too much? Did they think the coach was being unfair? Were they concerned about their playing time?*

This was a good way to keep things in the open and give teammates a chance to get things off their chests. It also allowed me to communicate better with the coach and keep him informed of what was going through the players' minds, although I was careful not to betray secrets or "snitch" on teammates.

■■■

One more thing...

Leadership must be earned. It isn't awarded, and it takes time to acquire, through practice habits and the way you conduct yourself day in and day out.

Leadership also is a given. Every team has it, the only question is whether it is positive or negative. Every team has players who naturally influence others by the force of their personality. But if the "negative" leaders are stronger than the "positive" leaders, problems arise.

Successful teams have leaders pulling in a positive direction, players who have the courage to stand up for what is right and are unselfish enough to look after the needs of their teammates.

Be one of those players!

TOUGHNESS

Mental toughness is absolutely crucial to becoming a successful player, and it shows up in so many different areas. Can you practice hard when you're not feeling well? Can you play through a minor injury? Can you come back from a major injury? Can you continue to work hard during drills that improve your skills but become tedious after awhile? Can you push yourself in the fourth quarter of a game when you're tired? Are you willing to work on your game during the summer when all your friends are goofing off and wanting you to join them?

These all relate to mental toughness and determine how good a player you will become. A lot of promising careers have died because players lacked the mental toughness to reach their potential.

Fatigue

No matter how well-conditioned you are, you're going to become tired during games, and you must learn to "play though it." You have to trick your mind into believing you can keep going. If you can do this, you can keep going.

This comes from experience. You will be amazed how hard you can work and how long you can play if you condition yourself, both mentally and physically. It is absolutely essential that you be in the best possible physical condition, but then you must work on mental conditioning too.

■■

STEVE: *My last two years at Indiana I averaged almost 38¹/₂ minutes a game. A lot of that came from working hard in practice. Not only did that enable me to be in excellent physical condition, but it conditioned my mind as well. In the NBA, I would see guys sit out of practices with a sore back or a jammed finger or a slightly sprained ankle. I had the attitude that I was going to play unless it was physically impossible. I didn't want anybody to take my job and I loved what I was doing.*

■■

Injuries

You have to be able to play through injuries, but this doesn't apply to severe injuries. You don't want to endanger your health by playing when you're badly hurt, and you aren't going to be able to contribute to the team if you are. Another healthy player will be able to perform better than you, so it is in the team's best interest to step aside and not try to be a hero.

Minor injuries, however, can be treated and then ignored during games. If you sit out when you can play, you let down your teammates.

All players suffer injuries, and if you play long enough you might suffer a serious one, such as a knee injury that requires surgery. The rehabilitation process is long and difficult, and requires the same sort of discipline that leads to successful play on the court. Although a major injury is never a positive thing, it can help build mental toughness that carries over into other areas of your game.

■■

ED: *I tore the anterior cruciate ligament and the cartilage in my knee my sophomore year in college. I didn't have reconstructive surgery, because they told me it might end my career. I had played in an exhibition game that prevented me from being able to take a redshirt year, so I couldn't just sit out and take a fifth year of eligibility. I had to get back as quickly as possible.*

To get to the place where I did my rehabilitation, I had to walk about 20 minutes across campus. A lot of times I did it in the morning, before classes. I'd be walking in freezing weather, knowing I was in for two hours of excruciating pain, thinking how great it would be to go back to a warm bed.

Then when I got there I was all by myself. Nobody would have known if I wasn't working hard. It would have been easy to sit back and let people feel sorry for me. Nobody knows what you don't do. But I took the workout the doctors had given me and tried to double everything. If I was supposed to do five sets of 10 repetitions of an exercise, I tried to do 10 sets of 20 repetitions.

I was able to come back and play much earlier than the doctors expected. We won our conference championship and we played in front of 30,000 people in the Metrodome in Minneapolis in the NCAA Tournament that season. None of that would have been possible if I hadn't worked as hard as I did in rehabilitation. Believe me, it was worth it.

■■■

Working out

Every player should have an individual workout program he or she follows throughout the year. Take a designed workout another player has used, or that a coach recommends (such as the ones in this book) and follow it.

A lot of players will do it for a week or two and then stop. They can't get through the pain. But after their mind and body become conditioned to it, they will see dramatic improvement in their performance. Hard work pays off. The challenge is to get through the hard work so you can reap its benefits.

You gain a toughness in the off-season that you can't get anywhere else. You're not born with it. A lot of players reach the level where it really starts to hurt, and they either stay there or regress. It's difficult to break through it and go to the next level.

You hear a lot of talk about fine lines separating great players from good players, or great teams from good teams. A lot of times that fine line is the pain threshold, or the toughness threshold. If you have the toughness to cross it, you'll have an advantage.

■■■

STEVE: *My freshman year in high school was really difficult for me. I averaged one point a game for the varsity team. I was up and down between the junior varsity and varsity teams and really had a difficult time. I still remember going into my dad's office and saying, "Coach, I want to be something very special. I don't want to be the average guy who goes through here and gets a letter jacket, graduates and comes back and hangs out at the high school football games. I want to be the best you've ever coached."*

He said, "That's fine, but I've heard that from a lot of players. I'll tell you what I told them. You've got to bust your tail during the summer. I'll give you a workout, and then it's up to you to do it. It's not a Monday-Wednesday-Friday thing. You have to do it every day."

He gave me a workout and told me not to come back for 14 days. During that time I had to do the workout every day for 14 days. I did it and went back to him, thinking I was done. He said, "Wait a minute, you've got 10 weeks left. This is the 14th of June, and we don't start school until the first of September."

That was really tough for me to get through. But I can go back and show you charts that show how my free-throw shooting improved, my ballhandling improved, my conditioning improved ... everything got better. The toughness I gained from those workouts not only helped me reach my potential, it enabled me to play 38 minutes a game in college.

Mental toughness also comes into play when you have to play back-to-back games during the season. This happens at every level. In junior high school, you might play two games in one day in a tournament. In high school you might play on Friday night and Saturday night. In college you might play three games in a week. In the NBA you might play four games in a week.

One of the most difficult things for an athlete is to come back and perform without much rest or preparation. If you have a great win on Friday night, you have to put it behind you and be ready to play again the next night. The same goes for a tough loss. If you lose a game you think you should have won, or if you get beat badly on a Friday night, you have to forget it and be ready to play the next night.

You have to be able to reach down. You have to have a resource of physical and mental strength that gets you through the difficult games. That's where workouts come in. Young players have a great opportunity to get into the habit of starting individual workouts at a young age, so that it becomes part of their routine.

The point is to be able to break through the "comfort zone." That's the purpose of a workout, whether it's weightlifting or running, where it really begins to hurt and you start to think of quitting. If you can train yourself to keep going, to break through that zone, you begin to develop a reserve of strength. It's like having money in the bank that you can withdraw when you need it. When it's late in the game and everyone is tired, if you have extra strength and mental toughness as a result of your conditioning program, chances are good that you'll come out ahead.

ED: *I've had guys ask to work out with me. They show up and they're gung ho, but by the end of the day they're dragging. They come back the next day, but tell you they can't make it tomorrow. After a week or two you can't find them and you're in the gym by yourself again.*

Failure

Failure is a learning experience for athletes if they respond to it properly. Nobody succeeds all the time. Nobody. The greatest players of all time have missed important shots, played poorly in big games and experienced slumps when they struggled over a period of time.

You are going to experience failure, so it's important to learn to deal with it.

Here again, mental toughness comes into play. You just have to keep going when things aren't going well. If anything, you should be motivated to work that much harder.

■■

ED: *Many times, especially at the high school level, teams that have the biggest heart rather than the biggest bodies have the most success. My senior year we didn't have a player taller than 6-foot-2, but I don't think we were ever out-rebounded. We finished the season with a 21-4 record and were one of the final eight teams left in the state tournament. We had great heart and toughness, and that allowed us to beat teams with more talent.*

STEVE: *We used to kid Dan Dakich, a teammate of mine at Indiana. We used to tell him he had the Big Ten Body of the Year. He was a little heavy and a little slow. He didn't have great skills. He was 6-foot-5 and couldn't dunk. But when we picked teams in the summer Dan would be the first guy we picked because nobody wanted to play against him. Those are the kinds of guys you want. They're tough mentally.*

■■

A final thought

Toughness comes down to whether or not you're willing to do more than what's expected of you. Everybody can do what the coach asks him to do. The thing that separates great teams and great players from the rest is how much they do that isn't expected of them.

The player who goes home after conditioning, or doesn't do anything in the off-season, will only go as far as his natural talent will take him.

The best thing about toughness is that it stays with you long after you're through playing basketball. A lot of the great coaches developed their toughness as players. Many successful businessmen developed their competitive edge from athletics. No matter what you do with your life after basketball, mental toughness will be an asset because it enables you to work harder than the next person.

ATTITUDE

Attitude leads to altitude. In other words, your mental approach to basketball will determine how high you go, as a player or as a team. This also is true for life outside of athletics.

If you watch the evening news, most of it is negative. That's the way our society has become. We focus on negatives and too often forget about the positive things. It's difficult to keep a positive outlook in the face of all these negatives, but it can be done.

As a player, you should make it a point to have the best attitude on your team and be positive. That's the kind of players coaches and teammates want. Nobody who wants to win wants to be around people with bad attitudes.

■■■

STEVE: *I was hired at a college in Indiana (Manchester) that had achieved only a few winning seasons in over 90 years. When I took over midway through the season, I told the players, "The only thing we're going to do differently right now is change your attitude. We're going to give you things to help you become better players, but the first thing we have to do is change your attitude."*

I looked at their record over the previous couple of years, and they were always in the game until the last few minutes, then they would end up losing by five, six, eight points. That's a sign of a poor attitude. They weren't risk-takers, and they weren't willing to step up and take the important shot. They didn't expect to win.

That's the best thing we've done: change the attitude. It's no more difficult to have a winning attitude than a losing attitude, and it certainly makes the game more enjoyable.

College coaches want players who want to be in the gym, who want to stop by and talk about basketball, who want to put in the extra effort. That's what they look for when recruiting. A player with a good attitude will always get a scholarship over a player of equal ability with a poor attitude.

■■■

If you love the game, the rest takes care of itself. Kids today have a lot of opportunities to get involved with basketball at an early age, but they don't always fall in love with it. Perhaps they've been forced into it by a father who was frustrated by his lack of athletic success. You've got to love the game to be successful.

Remember, you choose your attitude. You don't have to have a bad attitude about anything. You can't always control what happens to you, but you can control how you react to what happens. We all have 24 hours in the day, no matter how tall or skilled we are. We have 86,400 seconds in each day. What are you going to do with them? Are you a carer and a sharer, or a taker and a user? Will you use that time to build people up or break them down? Are you a helper or a hurter? Will you be part of the problem or part of the solution?

The answer to all these questions comes down to one thing: attitude. How do you react to a tough loss, or even a difficult practice? Do you come in with your head down, or are you talking enthusiastically about what needs to be done to get better?

■■■

ED: *I was the youngest head coach in the country, 22 years old, when I got my first job at Western Boone High School in Indiana out of college. The team won just five games my first year. I later took a job at Logansport High School and we only won eight games the first year, and we didn't win a single conference game.*

You have to have an attitude that enables you to get through difficult times like that, or you're never going to win. During my third year at Western Boone High School, we won 15 games and set the school's win record for a season. At Logansport, we won 16 games and a Sectional Championship only three years after that eight win season. We weren't that much better as players or coaches, but we learned to adjust our attitude, to look forward to the next day. We didn't worry about yesterday, and we looked forward to tomorrow.

What do you say when you wake up? Do you say, "Good morning, God!"? Or do you say "Good God, morning!"? The choice is yours.

STEVE: *Body language is important, too. I remember getting kicked out of practice by my father even though I had never said a word. But my body language was bad. I would roll my eyes or shrug my shoulders. The same thing happened to me in college. Unspoken reactions can infect a team, too.*

■■■

LEARN YOUR ROLE

One of the most difficult things for players to do is understand and accept their role. The higher the level of play, the more difficult it is. If the players who do not start, or do not play much, don't have a good attitude, the team will be affected.

In college, every player was a star for his or her high school team. But not everyone can be the leading scorer. Different players have to accept different roles. Someone is going to have to focus on defending the other team's best scorers, rebounding, setting up other players to score. Every successful team has players like that.

Roles can change during the course of a season. You might start out the season coming off the bench. Then midway through the season a starter gets hurt and you get to play more. If your attitude has been poor all along, you can't shift gears and suddenly have a great attitude. But if you keep a good attitude at all times, it's amazing how often that turns into something positive for you.

Roles also can change during a game. Perhaps you're the team's leading scorer, but the opponent makes defensive adjustments to shut you down. Suddenly you have to accept a different role, becoming a passer rather than a scorer. Or perhaps you're a point guard who concentrates on setting up scoring opportunities for other players. If the defense drops off of you, you have to be able to change your approach and hit shots.

It all goes back to attitude. Are you willing to do whatever it takes to win? Are you willing to take a charge? Dive on the floor for a loose ball?

Winners aren't born, they're created.

■■■

STEVE: *That was true for me in my NBA career. I had succeeded in college and came in with a lot of confidence. But suddenly I was fighting just to make the team and wasn't playing very well. I came down with a bad attitude. Then all of a sudden Brad Davis got hurt and I was thrown into the mix. I didn't make the most of the opportunity because I wasn't mentally prepared. My attitude wasn't what it should have been.*

Had I made the most of those opportunities when somebody got hurt, who knows what might have happened with my pro career? I wound up having a mediocre, four-year career in the NBA because I didn't have the same work ethic as a professional as I did in high school or college. It was my first experience of not playing, and I didn't handle it well.

■■■

DISCIPLINE

This area is very closely related to attitude and toughness. Discipline, it has been said, is doing something when it needs to be done and how it needs to be done, and doing it that way all the time.

If you're practicing a ballhandling move, for example, such as dribbling right to left behind your back, and you kick it out of bounds, what do you do? Forget it and try something else you know you can do, or go get the ball and do it again? A disciplined player chases the ball and keeps doing it until he or she gets it right.

Or if you're shooting free throws and you hit 80 out of 100 shots on Monday, do you take the next day off or do you try to hit more? If you hit 100 free throws in a row do you feel like you don't need to practice anymore, or do you try to hit the rim less often the next time? If you are an excellent ball handler going to the right but not the left, will you spend the time necessary to become as good going to the left? Discipline is understanding your limitations and progressing weekly and monthly.

Setting goals

Goal-setting is important, but you can't just set one long-term goal. You must have immediate goals, such as winning the next game or winning your conference championship. You don't just go from the bottom to the top in one step. You take one step at a time, and sometimes you have to go backward before you can go forward.

If you have a goal of winning a postseason tournament, you need to prepare during the season. Maybe you have two road games on consecutive nights. You might have to win back-to-back games away from home to win a postseason tournament, so use the experience during the regular season to prepare for that. If you're not disciplined during the regular season, you're probably not going to be disciplined after the season.

The same is true on an individual basis. Are you willing to follow a workout program, regardless of the weather or other distractions? If you have to go somewhere for the day, are you willing to get up at 6 a.m. and do your workout first, or do you take the day off? If it's 90 degrees outside, do you spend the day inside with the air conditioner or do you work out anyway?

During your workouts, you should have daily goals. Maybe you want to hit 60 percent of your jump shots and 80 percent of your free throws. Every day you should have a goal and keep track of your results. As you improve, raise your goals.

It can help to use your imagination while playing, particularly when you're by yourself. Younger kids do this naturally. They fantasize about going one-on-one with Michael Jordan and hitting the game-winning jumper before 20,000 screaming fans. Or hitting the free throw that wins the NCAA championship. This is a healthy thing as long as it motivates them to keep practicing.

Unfortunately, players tend to lose the ability to fantasize as they grow older. There is nothing wrong with using your imagination to make your workouts more fun and to motivate you to work harder and longer.

■■■

STEVE: *When I was going through my individual workouts, I would play games in my head. Like, "If I miss this free throw, we go home a loser." Or, "I have to hit the next five to get us within one point going into the fourth quarter."*

I was fortunate to be able to work out in a high school gym that seats nearly 10,000 people, because my dad coached there. I would be there by myself shooting, but I would pretend the gym was full and everyone was watching me. You have to put yourself in situations like that so you're prepared when it happens in a game.

■■■

Goal-setting also applies to playing in a pickup game. Do you just play, or do you have goals for yourself? Maybe you want to work on your post feeds, or on handling the ball with your left hand. There's always something you can work on when you play without sacrificing the team concept. Too many players only worry about shooting when playing in a pickup game, but that's only a fraction of the game.

Short-range goals are crucial to building toward the long-range goals. But intermediate and long-range goals help support short-term goals. If you lose two or three games in a row during the middle of the season, the fact you still can win a postseason tournament can keep you motivated. There's always something you can use for motivation.

It starts with discipline. It's hard to imagine that anyone doesn't have time to work on their game, even if they have a job during the summer. You can work out at 6 a.m., at noon, or at 10 p.m., whatever fits into your schedule.

■■

STEVE: *I remember the summer before my senior year in high school, I came home from a good workout at the high school gym at about 11 o'clock one night. I had hit 98 of 100 free throws and was really pumped up. One of the sources of my motivation that summer was James Blackmon, a player at another high school in our conference. Most people considered one of us to be the best player in the state.*

When I walked in the door and threw my dad's car keys on the table, I saw my dad lying on the sofa. I was hoping he would ask me how the workout went, because I couldn't wait to tell him how well it had gone. Instead he said he had just gotten off the phone with Blackmon's coach.

"What did he have to say?" I asked.

"Well, he said Blackmon just left his house," my dad said.

"What was he doing over there?"

"Oh, he just popped in to get the keys to the gym to go work out."

I was too young and naive to realize my dad was putting me on. I grabbed the keys and went back to the gym and worked for another hour. I look back, and those are the little things that got me over the hurdle of being an average athlete. I was so much more disciplined and determined than the majority of the athletes I played against.

■■

Even daily goals are important. How many free throws do you want to hit today? What percentage of your jump shots do you want to hit? Every time you start a workout, you should have a goal.

It all comes down to discipline, having those daily goals, having the short-range goals to point toward if the daily goals fall a little short, and having the long-range goals in the back of your mind to keep you going. That way, if you don't win those three games in the middle of December, you can still point toward your conference championship or the sectional.

The bottom line is your desire to improve. Are you willing to go back to the gym when you don't hit the number of free throws you want and shoot another set? If you're not the athlete you want to be, are you disciplined enough to go through the workouts to improve your jumping ability, your quickness or your strength?

You have to be willing to do it.

■■■

ED: *In high school, we used to play pickup games at 7 a.m. during the summer. After everyone went home, I stayed and did my individual workout. Then I went home and did my chores or whatever and went back to the park.*

That's where I met Rick Mount who was a three-time all-American at Purdue in the late 1960s, one of the greatest shooters who ever lived and the first high school player ever to appear on the cover of Sports Illustrated.

We played full court one-on-one for an hour or an hour-and-a-half, the best-of-seven games. It was a great opportunity for me to be with a guy who had that kind of discipline and work ethic. After we finished playing we'd sit down and he would share stories with me.

He used to tell me he was a lifeguard at the city park. He would work an hour and then get an hour off, all through the day. He would get 100 or 200 jump shots off every hour he played. When I heard that, I made it a point to get to the park early that night for the pickup games and get a couple hundred jumpers in before we played, because I knew if that's what it took for him to succeed, that's what I needed to do.

■■■

CONFIDENCE

Players must have confidence to play well, but to have confidence you must be able to play well. This is a dilemma similar to the classic argument of which came first, the chicken or the egg? Do you become confident first so you can play well? Or do you learn to play well so you can have confidence?

Actually, one feeds off the other. Your talent and confidence will grow together as you mature and improve. But there are things you can do to keep your confidence high, which in turn will help you play better.

It is important to remember, however, that you must keep your confidence in check. Confidence that grows into arrogance will hurt you, because you won't work as hard and you won't have enough respect for your opponent.

Having a healthy degree of confidence in basketball means that you know you can hit an important shot in a game, that you can handle the ball against defensive pressure or that you can stop an opponent from scoring. You must master the fundamentals first, of course, but confidence always comes into play. We all have seen players who have poor shooting form, but shoot well anyway. These players have confidence. Other players have great form, but don't shoot well. They lack confidence. The very best players, however, have done both: mastered the fundamentals and gained confidence.

■ ■

ED: *When I was in high school, I dribbled a basketball everywhere I went. By the time I was a senior, I dribbled two basketballs when I went to the park every morning. If it was during the school year, I carried my books in a backpack so I could dribble both balls. I didn't let myself make an excuse. If I walked to my girlfriend's house I dribbled two basketballs. Every place that I went, I was dribbling. Any type of dribble move you could imagine, I worked on along the way.*

When we played against Kentucky while I was in college, I went up against Ed Davender, who was rated by one magazine as the best defender in the nation. I didn't fear him nor did I lose the ball, because I was confident there was no way he could take the ball away from me. I had put too much time and effort into my ballhandling for that to happen.

STEVE: *When I went into the NBA, Karl Malone was one of the worst foul shooters in the league. Now he shoots better than 70 percent consistently. When you watch him, he mumbles something to himself. I don't know what it is, but you can bet it's the same thing every time and it's something that instills confidence.*

In my case, everybody wrote about how slow I was. I tried to feed off that as a scorer. I told people, "You're right, I'm a step slow, but I'm going to show you that you're two steps slow, because you're not going to stop me from scoring."

But it affected me as a ball handler. I was a point guard in high school but a shooting guard in college, so when I got to the NBA I had to go back to being a point guard. All of a sudden I had to go back to bringing up the ball against somebody like Derek Harper, and I didn't have confidence in that. I found myself throwing the ball to someone else to bring it up. It wasn't that my ballhandling skills had diminished, my confidence had suffered. And that just made things worse.

I remember one time Coach Knight called me aside in practice and asked me, "What do you think is more important? Going to the free-throw line knowing you can make it, or going to the free-throw line having the right mechanics?" I didn't hesitate. I said having the confidence you can make it. Because one coach might have a philosophy on what good mechanics are and another coach might have a different philosophy, if I know I'm going to make it, that's 75 percent of the battle. Too many players are thinking about their routine, their girlfriends, getting back on defense, or whatever, and because of that they don't hit their free throws.

■ ■

Remember, practice doesn't make perfect, it's perfect practice that makes perfect. If you don't play in a pickup game the way you need to play during the season, it won't help you. Or if you don't practice with the proper intensity, it won't help you. For example, if you go out to shoot around, but you shoot your jumpers casually and don't follow through properly and you walk after the ball, it won't help you during the game when you try to do it right.

Confidence is gained through playing at game speed for a long period of time. This is true whether it's practicing ballhandling, shooting or anything else. Over time, you gain the confidence that you can do it against anybody.

THE PHYSICAL GAME

All players, particularly guards, would like to be more athletic. Who wouldn't want to be quicker, a better jumper and stronger? You can be if you are willing to put the time and effort into it.

Nobody can guarantee that you will have a 40-inch vertical jump or be the quickest player in your league, because we all have different limitations. But you definitely can improve yourself physically. Like anything else important in your life, it's just a matter of devoting yourself to it.

This book presents workout programs that will improve your physical abilities (see pages 91 through 96). Make no mistake, it isn't easy. Nothing worth having is obtained easily. But as with any workout program, you have to go past your comfort level. If you do that, you will improve. This applies to lifting weights and to drills to improve quickness and jumping ability.

In this area, more than any other, mental toughness comes into play. The athletes who are mentally tough, who can withstand pain and push themselves to higher levels, are the ones who will improve the most physically.

FEET

You obviously can't play basketball without your feet, but too many players neglect footwork when working to improve.

If you want to improve your foot speed, you must "punish" your feet, both in drills and while you play in games. Always be sure to wear the proper shoes and socks, but you have to be willing to make your feet hurt. It's painless to be slow-footed while you play. But if you're willing to dig down and really move your feet and withstand some pain, your footwork will improve and your performance will reflect that dramatically.

Playing in a five-on-five pickup game actually promotes lazy footwork and can be detrimental to a young player's progress. You can get away with standing around and not moving your feet if there are nine other people on the court with you, and games of five-on-five always seem to wind up being a series of simple fast breaks because players don't get back on defense — particularly as they grow tired.

It's better to spend more of your time during the off-season putting yourself through drills and playing in half-court games of one-on-one, two-on-two or three-on-three, because more will be demanded of you in those situations.

When you do play in a full-court game, or a half-court game for that matter, make it a point to guard the other team's best player. Throw out a challenge. Say, "I'm going to try to stop you." Get that player motivated to be at his or her best, and that will make you be at your best.

Some young players are afraid to fail, but the off-season is the perfect time to fail. The games don't mean as much then, so you don't have to feel as much pressure to succeed. This is the time to improve your game. Take pride in "failing" by exposing the weaker aspects of your game and working to improve them.

This applies to something like foot speed. You can't wait until your "real" games in the winter to worry about whether or not your feet are quick enough. Work on this in the off-season by the way you play and practice.

Attitude comes into play here. If people tell you that you are slow, use that as motivation. Pound your feet when you play, and think about being quicker. It's better to be one step slow physically and one step quick mentally than to be one step quick physically and one step slow mentally. If the player guarding you is quicker than you but you are more alert mentally, he can't stop you because he doesn't know what you're going to do. You want to act, not react. Those players who act are quicker than those who react, regardless of their physical attributes.

It is best of all to be quick both physically and mentally. It is hard to say exactly how much quicker you can become through drills and by working your feet during games, but at least you know you are working harder than your opponents. That gives you an edge, because it gives you confidence. You're convincing yourself that you are quicker, and that alone can make you quicker.

But if you just sit back and say, "I can't jump," or "I've always been slow," that only makes it worse because you have the wrong mind-set. You're conceding defeat, and that can only hurt you. Say instead, "I might be slow right now, but I'm getting better." The mental side always improves the physical side, just as the physical improves the mental. They play off of each other and support each other. Put effort into both of them.

■■■

STEVE: *When I was a student at Indiana, Isiah Thomas was playing for the Detroit Pistons. Isiah came back one summer to attend summer school and joined us in our pickup games every day. I made it a point to guard him as often as possible. I didn't have much success; there was no way I was quick enough to stay with him. But it really helped me improve. I never had to guard anybody in my college career as good as he was.*

■■■

Many drills and workout programs are available to help players improve themselves physically. The bottom line of all of them, however, is that you have to be willing to keep working when it starts to hurt. It won't matter if you have the greatest workout program in the world if you aren't willing to put a high level of intensity into it. If you do it on a daily basis, you will improve. That much is guaranteed.

Blisters

Some players use blisters on their feet as an excuse for not working to improve their footwork. That's only an indication they haven't worked hard enough. If you work hard at your game your feet will become tough enough to withstand the "punishment" you put them through in your workouts and games. It's the players who take several days off at a time who have "soft" feet. Blisters are nothing more than an alarm that someone hasn't been serious about improving himself.

Proper foot care is important, because a player with bad blisters can't play, and might lose his or her spot to another player while sitting out. It's a simple thing, but very important.

EYES

All players obviously use their eyes when they play basketball. But that doesn't mean they use them correctly. Players, particularly guards, must be able to see the floor and understand what is happening at all times. An old saying among basketball coaches is that "many look, but few see." There is a difference.

Guards must keep their heads up at all times, of course, but there is more to it than that. They must know where the ball should go and where their teammates should be. You have to not only look, but see what is happening. If someone is posting up inside but doesn't belong there, he shouldn't get the ball. That is seeing, not just looking.

It also is important to know what kind of space you're working in. Do you know how long the court you play on is? How long is a regulation junior high school court? How long is a high school court? You should know this so that you can make the proper decisions at all times from anywhere on the court.

One of the worst things that has happened to basketball players is television and video games. Kids spend so much time staring at a screen that they get tunnel vision. They don't see anything else in the room, or, for that matter, think about anything else. If you're serious about becoming a good basketball player, you shouldn't spend much time with television or video games anyway. There are so many more valuable things you can do with your time.

Peripheral vision is crucial for all basketball players, but particularly guards. You can do some simple things to improve it, such as trying to see as many things as possible without turning your head as you walk down the hallway at school or down the street. Look straight ahead and see how far off to the side you can see. This simple exercise will help you take in more things and be aware of what is going on around you. You can train your eyes, just as you can train other parts of your body.

You also can practice outside at night or in a gymnasium, without much light, to force yourself to focus more closely. And consider playing pickup games, whether half-court or full-court, without going shirts and skins. This forces players to concentrate more on their surroundings and really see the other people on the floor, rather than blindly throwing a pass to someone who is dressed similarly.

Effective use of the eyes is most important in shooting. What do you look at when you shoot? The rim, sure, but where on the rim? The front? The back? Many coaches believe it is best to look directly over the front of the rim. You might prefer a different target. But you should have a target and focus your eyes there while shooting, rather than merely scanning the general area of the rim.

The same is true with passing. If you make a bad pass, ask yourself exactly what you were looking at. Were you looking at the specific area in which the player needed to get the ball?

■■■

STEVE: *When I was growing up, we had a goal in the driveway with a pole I had painted green. I used to practice dribbling to my right and passing the ball to the pole off the dribble. If I missed it, the ball would roll all the way down the street and I had to go chase it. I wasn't practicing no-look passes, I was looking right at the pole. This was a great drill to help me concentrate on my passing target, as well as improve my passing skills off the dribble.*

■■■

Good vision applies to defense, too. Defensive players must be able to see both their man and the ball. This is known as the "ball-you-man" theory. You should know where the ball is at all times, regardless of where your man is on the court. If you have good peripheral vision, you will be a better defender.

You also need to read the defense. How is your opponent playing you? Are they playing you to go to the left? Are they playing off of you and giving you an open shot? Many young players neglect to look and see how the defense is playing.

At higher levels, players need to be able to see how their defenders are playing them off of screens. Their positioning tells you what kind of cut to make, whether to curl or fade. The same is true for defending a pick-and-roll. You have to be able to read the defense and know whether to pass the ball to a teammate or take the ball to the basket yourself. All of this is related to using your eyes.

Baseball players have to see the ball well because it is so much smaller. A great hitter can't just stare in the general direction of the ball as it approaches the plate, he must focus on it tightly. Some of the best hitters can actually see the red seams on the ball as it spins toward the plate.

Steve visually locates the defender when he gets to the screener's shoulder.

A basketball is much easier to see, but that doesn't mean players shouldn't focus on it, or on the target toward which they are shooting or passing the ball. If you get a good look at the rim and really focus on it before you shoot, your percentage will improve dramatically.

■■■

STEVE: *When we used to take family vacations my Dad and I would play a game while we were riding in the car. We'd look ahead for highway signs and see who could read them first. It was a silly game, but it helped me focus my vision.*

ED: *My Dad and I used to play a game, too. He would lie in bed with a small bean bag. I would stand in the doorway. He would try to throw the bag through the doorway and I would try to stop it. If it went through he got a point and if I caught it or deflected it I got a point. He would fake and fake and that helped me with not only my reactions, but my eyes. That really helped me in basketball as far as getting deflections and steals.*

■■■

It might sound silly, but a good drill for young players is to take a ball, square up to shoot, and focus on the rim without shooting it. Just learning to concentrate on the rim is important for shooters. This is a good habit, because as you advance you will be shooting more difficult shots. You will be shooting a jump shot off the dribble, a turnaround jumper or a running layup — many times with a hand in your face — and if you have made a habit of really focusing on the rim, you will be a much better shooter.

Another good drill for eyesight and reactions is to have one player stand with his back to a player with the ball. On a voice command, the player spins around and tries to catch a sharp pass from the player with the ball — not just a chest pass, but a pass at the ankles or above the head. Try at least to get a hand on it, and then to catch it.

Obviously, all players should have their eyes checked to make sure their vision is correct. If you need contact lenses or glasses, get them. Then you can begin to work on seeing and not just looking.

It all comes down to gaining an edge. If you can see the floor a little better than your opponent you have an advantage, regardless of other physical limitations you might have.

HANDS

Hands are probably the most important physical asset a player has, other than a strong heart. You pass with them, shoot with them, dribble with them, rebound with them, even defend with them. Although footwork is crucial, your hands do the majority of the work.

Beyond that, the fingers are the most important feature of the hands, because they touch the ball first as you catch or grab it and touch the ball last as you release it.

There are an endless number of exercises you can do to strengthen your hands and fingers. If you're watching television, why not squeeze a tennis ball or small rubber ball to strengthen your hands and wrists? You can always be doing something to improve your game.

■■■

STEVE: *I used to do 25 fingertip push-ups every morning as soon as I got up. It became a habit, just like brushing my teeth. When I had study hall in high school, I would get a pass to go to the bathroom so I could do 25 fingertip push-ups; I didn't want to do them in front of everybody in the study hall. Just little crazy things like that can make a big difference.*

■■■

It isn't often mentioned, but strong hands are crucial to a player's performance. They make it possible to control rebounds, get off shots in traffic and handle the ball better. Many players are hindered because they have weak hands. It affects their shooting, ballhandling and everything else. This can be easily corrected with a little discipline and hard work. Strong fingers also help prevent jammed fingers, which have kept many players on the bench.

You should make sure to develop the hand you do not normally use in everyday activities. For most people this is the left hand. Use that hand when you eat or play a game such as pool or table tennis so that you become as comfortable with it as your dominant hand. Even doing something as simple as carrying your books or gym bag with your "off" hand can help develop it.

Keep this in mind while practicing or playing, even when you're by yourself. After you rebound a shot, dribble back out with your weak hand. You'll get in six or seven dribbles after each shot, which over time will make that hand much more effective.

When playing in a full-court pickup game, it's rare for anyone to apply full-court defensive pressure, so guards generally can dribble unchecked at least to the half-court line. Why not use the weak hand? You'll get in about 10 dribbles worth of practice every time down the floor.

The best players don't really have a strong hand or a weak hand because they have learned to use both equally. It is surprising to learn how many great players are ambidextrous. They might shoot with their right hand and eat or write with their left hand. Larry Bird and Rick Mount are examples. Being able to use both hands in basketball gives you twice as many options sometimes.

Good hands can make up for other physical limitations. If your hands are active when you play defense, that can make up for a lack of foot speed. Moving your hands to try to deflect the ball can enable you to pressure an opposing player while playing a step off of that player.

If you have five players on the floor with good hands, you can eliminate at least four turnovers a game. The ability to catch a bad pass or deflect a pass is a fantastic asset to have. Think about how many games are decided by three points or less. That's two possessions. That's two passes that are caught that might have otherwise been turnovers. Basketball is such a finely tuned game that a pass that is caught instead of being lost out of bounds can be the difference between winning and losing.

■■

ED: *Ron Harper, the NBA star with whom I played in college, had great hands. They were huge, strong and flexible. One time we were playing and Ron was streaking down the left side on a fast break. I threw a lob pass from midcourt that I thought was going to be way too high for him to catch. The band members were ducking because they thought the ball was sailing toward them. But Ron was able to barely catch the ball with both fingertips, control it and dunk it. Our fans went crazy and the other team had to call a time-out. That was the turning point in the game, and it was all because he was able to catch a bad pass.*

■■

Having a teammate with good hands gives the other players on the floor more confidence. If you're a guard bringing the ball downcourt on a fast break and you have two players running with you, you are more likely to throw the ball to the player with the best hands, if possible.

One drill to develop good hands is to have two players stand about 10 feet apart and throw a tennis ball back and forth. Make poor passes that are difficult to catch. The same thing can be done with basketballs. You can use two balls at once, with the players throwing a right-handed pass to each other at the same time, catching the ball with the left hand, switching the ball to the right hand, and passing again. This can be done rapidly to develop hand-eye coordination as well.

You also can use basketballs in drills with a third player. One player can pass to another, and the third player can bump the pass-catcher as he tries to control the ball and drive to the basket. This simulates a game situation that occurs often.

TOTAL BODY

Strength programs are an important part of all programs at higher levels of play. Virtually all professional and major college teams have some sort of organized, mandatory conditioning program their players follow.

Stronger players are better players. They can play longer without fatigue and a drop-off in performance. Simply put, a stronger muscle is better than a bigger muscle. It is important, however, to follow a program recommended by a qualified person and use the proper form in all exercises.

It used to be that players were discouraged from lifting weights because it was believed it would affect their shooting or overall finesse. This has been proven not to be true. Some of the greatest players in the game are muscular, and still shoot and handle the ball very well. Karl Malone of the Utah Jazz is a perfect example.

At what age should a player begin lifting weights? It varies because of different growth patterns, but it is never too early to begin a simple workout program. Anyone can do push-ups, pull-ups, sit-ups and other basic exercises that require little or no equipment and do not endanger the body. The *Pull-Up Trainer* is a machine that is excellent in producing strength without much risk of injury.

With a little imagination, any workout program can be made to be more enjoyable. With push-ups, for example, the placement of the hands can be varied to work different muscle groups. You can push off and clap your hands before you land to improve hand quickness as well. You can place your feet on a sofa or chair. Exercises such as these can be done almost anywhere, anytime.

Strength gives players confidence, not only on the court but off, and confidence is one of the best attributes an individual can have.

■ ■

STEVE: *My freshman year in high school I was 5-foot-10 and 125 pounds. When I graduated from high school I was 6-1, 155. And when I graduated from college I was 6-1, 180. Strength never was a problem for me. I never looked strong, but I was deceptively strong because I always did those little things.*

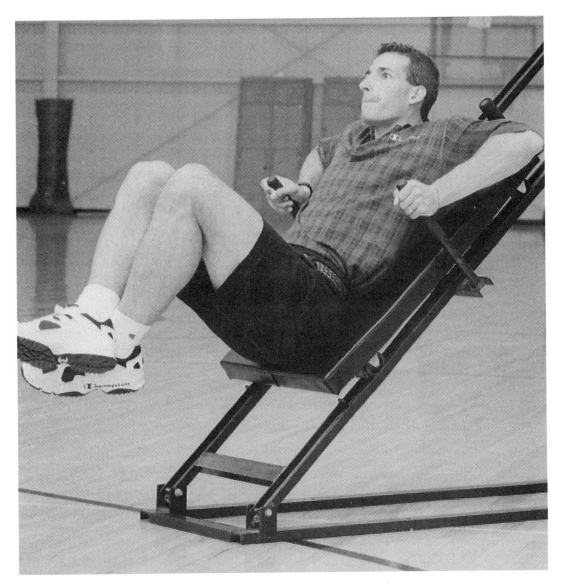

Above: Ed is using the Pull-Up Trainer. Natural strength training like pull-ups and dips are excellent, especially for athletes still growing because the chance for injury is decreased.

I did my fingertip push-ups every day. Sometimes I stood in front of a mirror and did tight curls, flexing my muscles as tightly as possible, moving my arms slowly. There's never an excuse for not making yourself stronger.

ED: *When I was young my dad bought me one of those pull-up bars that you put in the doorway to your bedroom. That was the only athletic thing he ever made me do, pull-ups every night.*

■■■

Regardless of your workout program, it's a good idea to shoot both before you begin and do some drills such as ballhandling after you finish. You want to have your body warm and your blood pumping before you lift weights or perform strength exercises. Afterward, you want to regain the flexibility lost by weight training. Why not spend the "cool down" shooting or performing light drills?

Stretching must be included in any strength program, both before and afterward. As with any exercise, be sure you are using correct form.

Keep in mind that strength is more important than weight, particularly for guards. You don't improve yourself by putting on weight if it is fat. Along those lines, all athletes — all people, for that matter — should follow a sensible diet. Cut out the junk food and fried foods and eat a lot of fruits and vegetables, along with bread and pasta. Be careful about how much caffeine and sugar you consume through soft drinks. You'll be amazed at how it affects the way you feel on and off the court.

Sleep also is important. Most people need about eight hours each night, but some need more or less. Many players in high school and college don't get enough, either because they are busy with other activities or they simply lack discipline.

You can't stay up past midnight and then get up early the next morning after five or six hours of sleep and expect to be at your best. It is good to make sound sleeping habits part of your routine early in life.

This is simply another way of allowing yourself to be the best you can be. If you are constantly tired, or if you do not eat a proper diet, you cannot perform at your best level.

HEART

"Fatigue makes cowards of us all." That's a saying Vince Lombardi, the great coach of the championship Green Bay Packers teams in the 1960s used, and it's true for all sports.

If you are tired, you cannot perform well. And every player must take the responsibility of being in shape. Your coach surely will include conditioning within the practice schedule, but what is stopping you from staying on the floor after practice and doing more work to improve your conditioning? When you run sprints, do you only try hard enough to make the required time, or do you run as hard as you possibly can? Too many players pace themselves and barely cross the line in the time the coach demands. If you settle for that you are cheating yourself and your teammates.

Do you only work hard when the coach is watching you or timing you? Or do you work as hard as you can all the time? The champions work hard because they want to do it, because they know they'll be better players for it.

The same philosophy applies when performing drills. If you do them at a high level of intensity, you'll improve your conditioning while improving your skills at the same time.

Just as with conditioning your muscles, conditioning your heart improves your confidence. If you see your opponent gasping for breath and bending over and tugging on his shorts, that should inspire you. If you're in shape you should be able to beat him. Set a goal of being in better shape than every player you face. Take pride in it.

■■

STEVE: *When I played at Indiana there were several games where I went the first 10 minutes of the game without scoring. But I averaged 22 points a game my final years, which meant I was scoring 22 points in 30 minutes. I wore my opponents down because of conditioning and endurance, and it related to the work I had put in during the summer.*

I was drafted by the Dallas Mavericks in the second round, the 26th pick overall, in 1987. They had several guards on guaranteed contracts, and their first-round pick, Jim Farmer, was another guard with guaranteed money. They really didn't have a spot for me on the team. I went to Billy Keller, who had been a great college and professional player in Indiana and asked him for advice. He told me to make sure I was the best-conditioned player in camp. I took that to heart and worked harder than I ever had. I won the mile-and-a-half race in training camp. Being in that kind of shape just gave me more confidence, and it carried over. I shot about 70 percent from the field in camp and played well overall. They ended up cutting a player with a three-year contract that guaranteed him $2.4 million to keep me, and it was largely because I was in great shape.

ED: *My senior year at Miami of Ohio the team went through a bad stretch of games and the other starting guard and I were benched because the coach wanted to go with younger players. I hardly played at all for awhile. I had a choice. Was I going to sit back and give up, or work harder? I decided to come in two hours before practice and work on my own to get better. By the time the other guys came in I had been there for two hours and was sweating through my practice gear.*

Before long one of the guys who was playing ahead of me, a freshman, ended up getting into trouble. All of a sudden I was back in the starting lineup and playing 40 minutes. I didn't miss a beat because I was in shape. My first game back I had the game-winning assist. The next game we played against Central Michigan, and they had a player named Dan Majerle. The game went into triple overtime. It was like two heavy-weight fighters going at it for 15 rounds. In the third overtime I stole the ball and raced the length of the court for the game-winning layup.

That happened only because I had spent the extra time to stay in shape. I had played all but 30 seconds in a triple-overtime game on the road after an eight-hour bus ride, but I was prepared to do just that.

■■

You can play games with yourself to test your limits. Say you decide to run a mile after your summer workout. As you finish the mile run, what if you ran another half-mile? Could you do it? Try it and see.

Or you can incorporate conditioning into your individual practice session. When you practice free throws, why not imagine it is the last two minutes of the game and your team is behind two points. If you miss one, "punish" yourself by running a half-mile or so. You'll condition your mind to perform at crucial parts of the game and you'll condition your body at the same time.

All players are going to "hit the wall" during a game at some point when fatigue starts to set in. But if you have conditioned yourself properly, both mentally and physically, you'll hit the wall so hard you'll go right through it. You'll keep going while your opponents fall back.

Another benefit of being in great shape is that it reduces your risk of injury. Common injuries or ailments such as shin splints, cramps and pulled muscles rarely happen to players who are in great shape.

Burned out? Never!

Sometimes people warn against burnout, but it is hard to imagine young players getting tired of a sport they love.

You can avoid this by getting involved in other activities, including other sports. Practicing basketball should be something you look forward to, not something you dread. If you take advantage of other opportunities you'll never dread playing basketball. And if you use some creativity during your workouts, you'll enjoy them. What could be more fun than being in the gym or in the park working on your game while your friends are out wasting time? You know you're gaining an edge.

Having fun isn't hanging out with friends doing nothing, although there's certainly a place in your life for socializing. Having fun is doing something positive for yourself. Some of the greatest days of your life will be the times you spend by yourself, working on your game. Imagine how many games you can win, how many times you can be the hero, when you're by yourself.

You have a choice. You can hang out with your friends every night doing nothing in particular or just lay around the house watching TV. Or you can work to stay in shape and improve your skills. Stop and think how you'll feel 30 years from now when you look back on your basketball career. Will you think, "Boy, I wish I had spent more time watching TV when I was a kid." Or will you wish you had worked harder to become a better player?

You know the answer. Do something about it before it's too late.

SKILLS

In some sports and activities, simply having a solid mental attitude and good physical ability is enough to facilitate success. Basketball, however, is not one of those sports. You must have skills in order to achieve in this game. You have probably seen individuals who look absolutely fantastic during layups, but never get into the actual game. They may be quality people who possess super physical ability, but if they don't have basketball skills they won't get playing time. Basketball is a game that demands skills — especially at the guard position.

In the pages that follow, we explain our philosophy, outline our techniques and provide drills to keep you off of the "All-Airport Team," and instead help you develop vital skills in the areas of ballhandling, moving without the ball, inside play, shooting, free-throw shooting, passing and defense.

BALLHANDLING

Ballhandling involves more than just dribbling the basketball. It includes catching the ball, passing it and just taking care of it without losing it.

Good ballhandling skills give you power as a player. If you can get anywhere on the court whenever you want, you can play at any level. Why is Muggsy Bogues playing in the NBA at 5-foot-3? It's because he can handle the ball and get where he wants to go almost anytime he wants to.

There is no excuse for poor ballhandling. If you are lacking in this area, it's only because you haven't practiced enough. And no matter where you are there is a surface you can dribble on, whether it's in the garage, on a sidewalk or in a parking lot.

All players should be able to dribble with either hand at a high rate of speed, and be able to change direction while dribbling. You don't need a lot of moves, though. A couple of strong moves, such as a crossover dribble or a behind-the-back move, are all you need, particularly at younger levels of play.

Think of dribbling like giving away money. With each bounce of the ball you're giving away more money. So you want to be efficient in your dribbling and do it no more than necessary.

There are only a few reasons to dribble the basketball:

1. To advance the ball upcourt.

2. To improve a passing angle or spacing.

3. To set or reset the offense.

4. To get by a defender for a shot.

If you are dribbling for any other reason you're wasting money. The fastest person in the world can't run faster than you can pass a basketball, so passing is usually preferable to dribbling.

Lateral dribbles are a waste of time and energy. You want to attack the basket at all times, even when reversing the ball. There's no reason to stand out front and pound the ball, going nowhere.

Eliminating unnecessary dribbling makes an offense more efficient. It's more difficult for the defense to stop you, and you improve your chances of scoring.

Many players attempt fancy ballhandling moves, such as dribbling between their legs or behind their backs. These moves have their place, but shouldn't be used by young players until they master the basics.

Left: Ed shows how to attack the defender's shoulder when driving by him by getting low and going right off his hip and shoulder.

The player with the ball should always attack the defender rather than turn his or her back on the defender and dribble aimlessly. Advanced players can be effective with their backs to the basket when they are close to the basket, but guards playing on the perimeter need to face the basket where they can shoot, pass or dribble. If you cannot advance the ball with the dribble, pass it to someone else.

Get down!

It is important to have your body in a crouched position while dribbling, because you have more explosiveness in your legs and you can protect the ball more effectively. Many players neglect this, especially when they get tired. But it's crucial to being able to control the ball effectively. If nothing else, there is less space between the ball and the floor for the defender to get a hand in and deflect it.

You also will be able to pass better from a crouched position. Basketball simply is not played from a straight-up stance, offensively or defensively. Guards, more than anyone, should keep this in mind.

To illustrate the importance of playing in a crouched position, imagine you were in a race over a distance of 20 yards, with $1,000 going to the winner. How would you start the race? Would you stand up straight or crouch down low? In basketball, you are trying to beat another player to a spot on the floor with a quick burst of speed. It's important to have a low center of gravity, like a sprinter coming out of the blocks.

This brings up another drill. Have somebody time you as you sprint the length of the court as fast as you can. Then have yourself timed while dribbling the ball with your "strong" hand and again while dribbling with your "weak" hand. This will point out very clearly how well you dribble, particularly with your "weak" hand.

Beating the defender

All ballhandling drills should be performed with high intensity. It does you no good to perform a drill at half-speed, because you won't be playing in a game at half-speed. If you kick the ball away, fine, that's how you improve. Just keep working, at full speed, until you master the skills.

An excellent drill for young players is to play one-on-one with a limited number of dribbles allowed before you have to shoot. For a grade school or junior high school player, perhaps three or four dribbles would be a good number. A more advanced player would be allowed just two or even one dribble.

If you can't create a good shot for yourself in a few dribbles, you're not going to get it done. It does absolutely no good — in fact it's a bad habit — to pound the ball and pound the ball without really going anywhere with it.

Leave question marks

A common mistake among ball handlers is to try to get by the defender by dribbling wide around that player. Go off the defender's shoulder in the most direct line possible

Left: Ideally, you want to switch places with the defender. If you can execute the "question mark" and not the "comma" you get the defender on your back.

then get him on your back. If you hit the defender's shoulder as you go by, fine. If a foul is called, it probably will be called on the defender. In order for a charge to be called, the contact must be taken in the torso after the defender has established legal guarding position.

Think of it this way: draw a question mark with the path you take, not a comma. If you take a more direct path — a question mark — you can beat your man and create an advantage for your team. A path like a comma allows the defense to recover.

Exploding toward the basket from a crouched position makes up for any lack of quickness you might have. A player with average quickness can get by a quicker player by using the proper fundamentals. You have the advantage because you know when the race starts. The defender has to react to your movement, and is moving backward.

Effective ball handlers create assists with their dribbling skills. Most assists are not great passes but simple passes created by the offensive team's advantage in positioning. If you can draw another player's defender toward you by beating your defender off the dribble, you can make a simple pass for an easy shot.

If the ball handler can go by his defender, he creates help from other defenders which in turn gets a teammate a shot and gets the passer an assist.

■■

ED: *When I was a senior in high school I dribbled two basketballs everywhere I went. I lived close enough to school to walk, and I always dribbled two basketballs along the way. The same was true when I went to the park or anywhere else.*

I also liked to challenge teammates before practice started. Once in a while, when I was dribbling a ball before practice, I would steal a ball from a big man and challenge him to steal either one of them from me. I'd be dribbling around the court with two basketballs and some big guy chasing me. They'd get mad because I had their ball, but I had fun with it. Eventually they'd steal it or I'd give it back to them, but it helped improve my dribbling skills.

STEVE: *I used to dribble a ball around our yard at home. The neighbors thought I was crazy, but it really helped me. The ball would hit a bump in the yard or an acorn that had fallen from a tree. Being able to control the ball when it's taking weird bounces helps improve your skills.*

I dribbled through a rock bed one summer to improve my fingertip control. And I had one ball that had a knot by the valve stem. Whenever that part of the ball touched the ground it would take a strange bounce. If you can learn to control a ball like that you certainly can control a regular ball.

■■

Keep your palms clean

The ball should be dribbled with the fingertips, not the palm of the hand. You cannot control the ball effectively if it touches your palm.

If you are playing outdoors, on an asphalt court, in your driveway or on a dirt court, it's easy to tell if you have dribbled correctly. The palm of your hand should be relatively clean, while the fingertips will be dirty.

Scott Skiles, a veteran NBA point guard, tells the story of when he was a kid playing on a dirt court. His father would check his palms every day when he went back into the house to see if his palms were dirty. If they were, his dad knew he had been fooling around and not using proper fundamentals.

Skiles tried to outsmart his dad by going down to the lake by their house and washing off his palms before going inside, but he realized later he hadn't fooled anyone.

The finer points

Dribbling is a relatively simple action, but certain fundamentals apply.

It's crucial to keep your head up while dribbling so that you can see the floor. If you dribble with your head down, you'll get yourself in trouble because you won't be able

Left: When dribbling utilize the finger pads (finger tips) not the palm.

Right: Ed executes the pullback dribble. Notice that the ball is even with and behind the back knee for protection and control.

to see another defender coming over to help or a teammate who might be open for an easy basket.

The ball should not go above your thigh while dribbling. Some great ball handlers such as Magic Johnson dribbled higher, but he had unique physical gifts that enabled him to do so. Younger players need to keep the ball low. An exception is a "speed dribble" in which you are dribbling downcourt for a layup as fast as you can with nobody guarding you.

When executing a crossover dribble, the ball should be passed from one hand to the other below the knee. This forces you to keep a low center of gravity and makes it more difficult for defenders to deflect the ball. Snap the wrist as you cross the ball and take a long, strong stride past the defender toward the basket. Don't go sideways.

If you dribble behind the back, pull the ball back sharply and snap it forward quickly. You might even slap your butt as you do so to help ensure a crisp move. Make sure you go somewhere, however. There's no point in taking the ball behind your back several times without going forward with it. That's nothing more than showing off.

When dribbling between the legs, take a long stride while keeping a low center of gravity and push the ball forward, not sideways. That helps you — forces you, actually — to get by the defender.

An inside-out dribble is effective for advanced players. It can be practiced on a gym floor or outdoor court with a line. Dribble the ball on the line a few times, then take it with the right hand and dribble across the body outside of the left foot, and then explode by the defender while dribbling back to the right. Just practicing the drill improves ballhandling and control.

A pullback crossover dribble is one of the most effective ways to beat pressure defenses. If you have two defenders coming toward you or if you're having difficulty getting by your defender, you can pull the ball backward two dribbles, keeping the ball even with and behind the backs of the knees, and prepare to cross over. Now you have the defender(s) coming toward you and you can attack the defense and get by it.

Changing speeds while dribbling also can shake loose a defender. When facing pressure defense it often isn't how fast you dribble, it's keeping them off balance. If you slow down or hesitate, thus making the defender slow down, you can cut sharply and work yourself free. This negates an advantage in quickness the defender might have.

Spin moves are not recommended for young players, but are great when trying to shake loose a defender around the baseline. Again, keep your center of gravity low and keep the ball as low as possible. Pull the ball until your body is between the ball and the defender, then switch hands. This reduces the risk of losing possession to a defender and makes it a relatively safe move. It's best used on the baseline. If used in the open court, it's too easy for another defender to anticipate your movement and deflect the ball while your back is turned.

It also is important to have a counter move for every move that you have. If the defender takes away your favorite move you need to have an alternative. For example, if you like to fake one way and use a crossover dribble to go the other way, the defender eventually might anticipate and position himself to cut off your crossover. In that case you need to be able to simply blow by the defender without a fake.

Younger players should master the fundamentals of ball control before attempting the more difficult moves. Learn to walk before you run.

Be creative

There are many things you can do to help you improve and also make your practices more fun.

Young players might want to consider wearing an old pair of glasses with tape across the bottom halves of the lenses. This prevents them from looking at the ball while dribbling. Dribbling at night when you can't see the ball also helps — as long as you're in an open area where you won't collide with anything. When playing outdoors in the winter, don't worry that wearing gloves will ruin your practice. That can help improve ballhandling skills as well.

When you see a great player with a move you admire, work to acquire the same move instead of just sitting back and admiring it. Envision yourself in that player's uniform, playing before thousands of people in a big game. Use your imagination to help motivate yourself to work harder and make it more fun for yourself. Great players aren't born with great ballhandling moves, they've worked hard to develop them.

Drills

The following are some drills you can use to improve your ballhandling skills.

Zig-Zag Drill

This is a good drill for beginners, but it also acts as a "refresher course" for more advanced players.

Start at the baseline in the corner of the court. Dribble to the foul line, then to the sideline, then to midcourt. Dribble the length of the court, using about one-half the width of the court. Always use the outside hand — the right hand when moving toward the right and left when moving left. Incorporate various moves when you change directions, such as crossover and behind-the-back dribbles.

The Chill Drill

Start at the left side of the court where the baseline and sideline meet. Hold the ball in your right hand. Execute an inside-out move. (Dribble twice on the line in front of you. On the third dribble, take the ball across your body and bounce it to the left of the line in front of your left foot. Explode past an imaginary defender by pushing off your left foot and pushing the ball in front of you back on the line, trying to cover as much ground as possible. Keep your knees bent and your body on the line, moving only the ball. End at position A.)

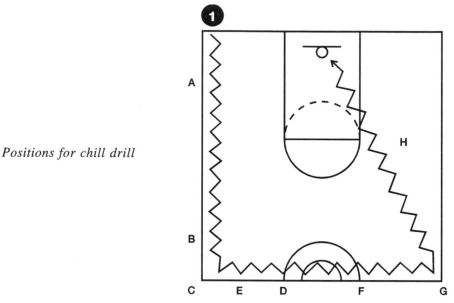

Positions for chill drill

Repeat the inside-out move at point B. (Keep in mind that the ball stays in the right hand.)

Come to a quick jump stop where the sideline and halfcourt line intersect (position C). Execute a reverse or spin dribble, keeping your left foot on the ground. Make sure to reach (hook) with your right leg in order to beat the defender. Pull the ball, being careful not to palm it, as you get the imaginary defender on his back, then switch the ball to your left hand and dribble quickly to position D.

At point D, pull the ball back beside your left knee, execute two low, quick retreat dribbles until you reach position E. The retreat steps help create space against a trap or double-team.

At position E, execute a quick, low crossover dribble, switching the ball to your right hand.

Take two dribbles and come to a quick jump stop at position F. Execute a half-a-spin move, which is the counter move to the reverse or spin dribble. Do this by pivoting 180 degrees on your left foot and pull the ball until it is directly in front of your right foot. Bounce the ball with force in front of your right foot when your back is to the defender. Then explode out by pivoting on your left foot.

Plant your right foot where the sideline and halfcourt line intersect (position G) and execute a behind-the-back from your right hand to your left hand, trying to cover as much ground as possible by pushing off your right foot toward position H.

At position H, execute a stutter-step to freeze the defender and make a quick, be-tween-the-legs dribble move, switching the ball from your left to your right hand. Make one hard dribble to the basket for a layup with your right hand.

You should also practice this drill starting with your left hand so that moves can be perfected with both hands.

Kill the Grass

Go inside one of the circles on the court — at midcourt or a foul circle — and pretend you are standing in grass. Dribble around the circle and try to "kill the grass" while using various dribble moves. Be creative, even fancy. Go for 60 seconds as hard as you can.

Up Two, Back Two

Do this for 30 seconds and try to build up to a minute. Take two dribbles forward, two dribbles backward and then snap a crossover dribble to the other hand. Then go two forward, two backward and snap a crossover to the original hand. Try to cover as much ground forward and backward and protect the ball as you would if you were being closely guarded. This is an excellent drill to prepare you for facing pressure defenses.

Two Ball Dribble

Start by simply dribbling two balls at the same time in rhythm so they both hit the floor at the same time. Then dribble so that one ball is up while the other is hitting the floor. Then dribble one high while dribbling the other low. As your skills improve you can dribble one behind your back and cross over with the other one. Try dribbling both balls in a figure eight between your legs. See how many laps you can make without fumbling the ball. Try to come up with a variety of combinations that will improve your skill.

Attack Drill

You can do this one with a partner. Dribble toward each other as hard as you can, then execute a crossover dribble at a predetermined spot and graze each other's shoulders as you go by. Then do it with a behind-the-back dribble or other move.

Dribble Tag

You can do this with one or more partners. Designate an area, such as the center circle, free-throw lane or midcourt, depending on how many people are involved, and try to deflect each other's balls while dribbling. Keep moving, protect the ball and go after someone else's ball.

Stationary Drills

You can perform many ballhandling drills while standing still. These are drills that can be performed anywhere, even in your bedroom.

The *figure-eight drill* is one of the most common of all ballhandling drills. Simply crouch low and move the ball around the outside of one leg, through the legs, around the other leg, and back through the legs. Do it in one constant motion, as quickly as you can.

You can perform a variation of the figure-eight drill by dropping the ball to the floor and catching it every time it passes through your legs. You also can dribble the ball around and through your legs rather than passing it.

In *single leg circles*, move the ball from hand to hand around one leg as quickly as you can. You also can do *double leg circles*, keeping your feet close together and moving the ball around both legs.

To perform *body circles*, move the ball around your body, starting at your ankles and gradually moving upward to your head, then back down again.

Conditioning, too

You can incorporate conditioning with ballhandling in several ways. You can simply dribble the length of the floor and back as fast as you can. Do it with each hand, and with two balls at once. You want to push the ball as far ahead of you as possible without losing control. As always, control the ball with your fingertips, not the palms of your hands. And keep your head up!

Try dribbling the lines on the floor sometime, tracing every one of them. Start at one corner on the baseline, dribble to one foul lane, up to the free-throw line, across the lane, down the lane to the baseline, to the corner, up the sideline and so forth. Use speed dribbles, hesitation dribbles and other skills along the way. Change hands every time you get to an intersection. Do it with two balls. Think of other things you can do to make it more fun and challenging. Make several laps at a high rate of speed.

You also can incorporate shooting the basketball with your ballhandling drills. Dribble hard to a spot on the floor, pull up and shoot. Run to get the rebound, dribble the length of the floor with the "weak" hand and take it all the way for a layup. Rebound, dribble to the other end and shoot a three-pointer. Imagine you are being double-teamed and make moves to beat defenders. Be creative and have fun with it.

Try dribbling in place with one hand for a certain length of time, such as five minutes. You might be surprised how tired you'll get, but you'll build your dribbling muscles along with your skills. You'll improve your fingertip control and condition your forearm. When you get into a game against a team that presses full court, you'll be prepared.

The key in drills such as these is to push yourself beyond your comfort zone. If you never lose control of the ball, you're not doing it quickly enough. And continue with drills when you are tired to simulate game situations. If you are accustomed to working hard at drills, you won't get as tired during a game.

Many other ballhandling drills are available to help you. See if you can make up some of your own.

MOVING WITHOUT THE BALL

Point guards will have possession of the ball more than any other player, but other guards — and all players, really — need to be able and willing to move without the ball.

Most players, including point guards, only have the ball in their hands a fraction of the time during a game, so it obviously is important to know what to do when you don't have it. And if the players without the ball are active, they make life much easier for the player with the ball.

Moving without the ball is vital for great shooters. You create shots for yourself by what you do without the ball more than what you do after you get it. It's great to be able to drive by someone for an easy basket, but most of the time you need to shake loose from a defender when you don't have the ball by faking or coming off a screen.

It isn't enough to move for the sake of moving, however. You have to move with a purpose. You don't go on a trip without having a destination in mind, and the same thing applies on the basketball court. Know where you're trying to go and what you're planning to do when you get there, whether it's to get open for a shot or set a pick for someone.

Never hesitate to set a pick for someone. It might sound strange, but screeners get open more often than the player for whom the screen is set because the defense usually focuses on the player receiving the pick rather than the one setting it. The more you screen, the more you'll be open. Perhaps the single most effective move to get open is to screen and then move directly into a cut. The defender usually doesn't have time to react to this maneuver, particularly if that player leaves you to guard the teammate coming off of the screen.

Know Where to Go

Your movement depends on your offensive system, of course, but it's important to keep some basic rules in mind. You must be aware of how your defender is playing you. You'll usually want to fake one way and then cut another to get open. But if the defender isn't keeping his eyes on the ball, you probably can stand in one place for awhile and get a pass for an easy shot. Keep this rule in mind: "Take a man low to go high, take a man high to go low and take a dummy nowhere."

The most common cut is a *V cut*. You move in one direction to set up your defender, then cut sharply at an angle to get open. Change of speed also is a vital element of moving without the ball. You can walk your defender in one direction, then cut sharply to get open. If you move slowly your defender will too, and that makes it easier for you to get open. It also negates any advantage in quickness your defender might have. Remember to keep your hands up so you can receive a quick pass, and be careful not to push off with your hands.

Using the screen and reading the defense: Notice that Steve gets to the screener's shoulder and sees the defender.

ED: *I used to practice V cuts in the house as I was walking through it. Or if I was turning a corner, I would make it a point to plant my foot and push off. It got so I would execute V cuts in a game without even thinking about it.*

A *tight cut* is used when your defender is following close behind you. You can cut hard off the screener and curl toward the ball to get open, in the shape of a U. Remember, a tight defender calls for a tight cut. You determine what cut to use when you get to the screener's shoulder.

A *flare cut* is used when your defender tries to fight over the top of a screen and to meet you at the wing arc. Instead of making a U-turn, you flare out away from the defender while the defender is fighting over the top of the screen.

The defense might switch off of a screen, which means you'll have a new person guarding you. It might be a taller player, which opens up new options for you, such as taking that person farther away from the basket.

Steve executes the V cut. Note that he plants his left foot with the body crouched after taking the defender to the basket before cutting to the ball.

Right: the defender follows Steve, so Steve executes the "tight" cut.

Steve executes the "flare cut."

Steve gets into good shot preparation after executing the "flare cut."

■■■

STEVE: *There's an art to cutting, and it can be a great deal of fun. I played against some great defenders in college and in the NBA, but I never felt like anyone could deny me the ball. I had the confidence I could always get open if I read the defense correctly and made good cuts. The next step is being able to get off a shot quickly after catching the ball in a good position. You should know what you're going to do with the ball before you catch it.*

■■■

Be in Shape

Conditioning is vital to moving without the ball. You must be in top shape to stay active throughout the game. This alone will give you an edge. If you're in better shape than the person guarding you, you can easily get open by staying on the move and making sharp cuts.

If you work your feet and legs hard during practice, making them as strong and quick as possible, you will reap the benefits during the game.

Players shouldn't shy from contact with their defenders. If you have some contact, you can read the defender's movement that much more easily and make a sharp cut to get open. You can push off slightly with a subtle elbow to help you, but be careful not to commit a foul.

You also should make contact with the person screening for you. Bump the screener's shoulder as you cut to make it more difficult for the defender to stay with you. If you get to the screener's shoulder before the defender does, you will get open for a pass if you read the defender and curl or fade accordingly. Set up your defender with a fake, then make a sharp cut for the screener's shoulder. This isn't commonly taught, but it can get you open. If you get to the screener's shoulder, now all you need to do is make the correct read and you will be open.

■■■

STEVE: *I had some great screeners when I played at Indiana, guys like Todd Meier, Daryl Thomas and Brian Sloan. It wasn't uncommon for me to go up to them after a game and ask them how their shoulder felt. I wanted them to have a bruise or two, just as I should have been bruised. That meant we were executing the screens properly. Your teammates will take pride in it too. Cutting and screening are contagious.*

■■■

Footwork and balance are crucial elements in getting open without the ball. If a slight bump from a defender knocks you off balance, you'll have a great deal of difficulty getting open. At higher levels of play, defenders are taught to bump cutters to slow their cuts and knock them off balance. Offensive players need to be able to contend with this.

A player can't keep his eye on everything going on during a game, of course, so if you have to lose sight of something while moving without the ball, lose sight of the ball first. Don't lose sight of your defender. When you catch the ball, you must know where you are on the floor and where your defender is. If you know those things at all times, it makes it much easier to know what to do after you catch the ball.

It's a good idea to look at your opponent while cutting. Look him or her in the eye when you can. Get to know that player well so you never lose sight of him.

Peripheral vision comes into play while moving without the ball. If you can know where the ball, your defender and the screener are all at once, you have a great advantage.

Study the Game

You can study moving without the ball by watching games, whether it's in person, on television or on film. Watch a player without the ball, particularly a guard who is expected to score, and see what he does to get open. You can always learn something new by studying games as you watch them.

You'll notice that players who are most successful at getting open without the ball don't waste effort. They don't try to run from their defenders or play hide-and-seek, they read the defense and make sharp cuts. They use change-of-pace, sharp V cuts and make use of screens — either coming off of them or setting them.

If you play at the high school or college level and have access to video tapes of your opponents, take advantage of them. Use them to study players who will be guarding you, and learn what they like to do so you can come up with something to counteract it.

Playing with a Purpose

You can work on your movement during pickup games in several ways. For example, assign yourself limitations, such as making sharp cuts and catching the ball twice before you can shoot it. Make yourself work harder than is absolutely necessary to get open.

If you can learn to get open without the benefit of a screen, it's much easier to get open when you do get screens during a game.

You can even use defenders as screeners. If you are being guarded by more than one defender, you have created an advantage elsewhere on the court. This also applies to box-and-one or diamond-and-one defenses where one defender follows a team's best offensive threat while the rest of the team plays a zone.

■ ■

STEVE: *After my sophomore year in college at Indiana, coach Knight took me aside and told me I was going to start practice the following season on the White team with the nonstarters. He didn't think I was one of the best five defenders on the team, and he wanted to go with his five best defenders.*

I used a little reverse psychology, however, and tried to turn the tables. If coach Knight was telling me these other five guys were the team's best defenders, I was going to try to see if any of them could guard me. Not only did I work harder on my defense while with the White team, I worked harder on offense to score against our "best" defenders.

I even told the players on the Red team what was going on. I said that the coach had put me with the White group because he thinks you're a better defender than I am, so prove it. I had one of the best stretches of practice ever during that week, shooting as well as ever. It really got to coach Knight because he was trying to prove a point and I was lighting up his great defenders.

He finally got the last word by calling for another five-on-five scrimmage. But he said, "Everybody on the White team can shoot except Alford." I had to laugh and he did too, a little. But I was always looking for reasons to motivate myself to move well without the ball.

■■

Drills

Perhaps the best drill for moving without the ball is to set up a couple of chairs on the floor. You can also do this drill on an outdoor court without chairs.

Pick a spot on the floor or court and place a chair or other object with its back to the basket. A good place to start is at each elbow, extended from the foul line at an angle to the basket. Put a ball on one chair. Make a V cut to one chair, touch it, then cut sharply to the chair on which the ball has been placed, grab it and shoot it without dribbling. Don't shoot behind the chair. Pick the ball up in one sweeping motion and take a step beyond the chair. Follow your shot and hit a layup if you didn't score. Then place the ball on the other chair and repeat the drill.

This drill teaches you to make a sharp V cut and shoot turning into each shoulder. It's important to learn to cut in all directions and be able to shoot while moving toward the right or left.

This drill will improve your conditioning and hand-eye coordination. Take 10 shots, then work up to 15 and more. Always cut hard.

Picking up the ball from the chair before shooting might be difficult at first, but make sure you bend over to do so. Don't try to do it standing up straight. Also make it a point to stay within your shooting range. As you get older and become more comfortable with the drill, you can place both chairs behind the three-point line.

Continue to challenge yourself by incorporating dribbling and shot fakes into this drill. Pick up the ball, dribble hard to the right or left and shoot it. Throw in a shot fake at times. Again, use your imagination to simulate game situations.

You can do this drill without a chair or other object on which to place the ball. You can cut, bounce the ball hard at the elbow, cut to the other side and back and pick up

The Chair Drill

Step One: Set up two chairs with a ball in each chair (top).

Step Two: Touch one chair making a V cut by pushing off with the inside foot and cut to the other chair (above).

Step Three: Pick the ball up from the chair while squaring up to the goal and shoot (left).

the ball before shooting. Even if you have to lay the ball on the floor or pavement, this drill can be effective.

Add variety by replacing the chairs with a teammate. One player takes the ball and dribbles and shot fakes while the other makes a sharp cut off an imaginary screener. The cutter must catch the ball in a position squared up to the basket, ready to shoot, without traveling.

It is also good to do the drill without actually shooting the ball. After one player catches the ball, he shot fakes and dribbles while the other player cuts and receives the pass. This is a great conditioning drill because it incorporates a lot of sharp cuts.

INSIDE PLAY

Guards should learn post skills just as taller players do. This adds another element to an offense and makes your team that much more dangerous. A guard who can post up and score around the basket creates all sorts of problems for defenders. One of the greatest compliments you can receive is being told that you have a complete game. Don't limit yourself by not having an inside game.

When you're playing around the basket, you must use different senses. You see more by feeling your defender and reacting accordingly. For example, if your defender is playing three-quarters defense by standing alongside you and placing one arm in front of you, place an elbow in the armpit of the defender's other arm and assume a wide base by spreading your legs.

Use your free hand as a target for the player with the ball away from the defender to make it easier for him to pass to you. Catching the pass is your responsibility, not the player passing the ball. First "catch" the ball with your eyes by locking onto the pass and following its path. If you take your eyes off the ball, you are more likely to fumble it. You can hold off the defender with your arm under his or her armpit without drawing a foul to make it easier to catch the pass.

Once you catch the pass, tuck it under your chin with your elbows out. Keep your butt low and knees bent. Your goal now is to switch positions with the defender. You want to have your body between the defender and the basket. This may be accomplished by executing a drop-step, a quick spin, a Sikma move, or an up-and-under move.

These three things — the catch, protecting the ball with your elbows out and feeling your defender's position — should happen almost simultaneously as you gain experience. If the defender is playing you on the baseline side, for example, you can hook him or her with a drop-step as you turn toward the basket, freeing yourself for an easy shot.

You can practice this with a partner or even by yourself. Catch the ball, position it under your chin with your elbows out and execute a drop-step. Do it on both sides of the lane.

If the defender plays you in a three-quarters position on the top side, you would drop-step to the baseline side with your shoulders parallel to the backboard so that the defender has to go through you to get to the ball.

If the defender plays behind you and does not make contact, initiate contact by backing in as close to the basket as possible. After you feel contact, you can react accordingly.

If the defender is playing straight behind you but making only slight contact, use a fake to throw the defender out of position one way or the other, and then make the appropriate move.

If the defender is pushing you hard with a forearm or chest — you see this often at higher levels, particularly in the NBA — you can execute a quick spin. Lean your shoulders backward on the defender and pivot around him. Use a low dribble so it is difficult to steal. If you are on the right side of the court (from the perspective of facing the basket), you would catch the ball with your back to the basket, pivot on your left leg, move your right leg around the defender and point it toward the basket.

If the defender releases contact as soon as you catch the ball, you can make what is commonly known as a "Sikma move," named after former NBA player Jack Sikma, who popularized it. Simply reverse pivot, pulling one leg backward, and turn and face the basket while moving the ball above your eyes. That serves as a shot fake and might get the defender in the air, allowing you to move toward the basket. If the defender backs off too much, you can simply shoot the ball.

You also can front pivot by moving one leg forward, spinning around and facing the basket. Kevin McHale of the Boston Celtics used this move effectively. After you have squared up and are facing the basket you can execute a variety of moves to score.

If you are fronted by the defender — which often happens to guards who are posting up — you have a couple of options. You can walk the defender up the lane, put one leg in between the defender's legs, put both arms in the air and look for a lob pass.

Even better, jump into the lane underneath the net. The defender must turn and find you — otherwise you would be open for a layup — at which point you use a swim technique to get open. Move one arm around the defender's back and slip one leg around the defender and call for the ball.

These are basic post moves that require practice to execute. They are very valuable, even for guards, and make you that much harder to guard. Practice them with a defender. The defender doesn't have to be an active player, just somcone who can position himself in a certain way so you can react correctly.

You can't expect to stand still and get open. You must move and set up your defender to provide a passing angle for your teammate with the ball. Many guards are not good post defenders because they have not been taught properly. Learning some basic post moves gives you an advantage.

Don't forget that you can pass out of the post. In fact, one of the best ways to get someone open for a perimeter shot is to work the ball into a post player, let the defense react and pass the ball back out. Guards in particular should be able to pass the ball from a post position, because a taller defender might help your defender and prevent you from getting a good shot.

■■■

STEVE: *We won the NCAA championship in 1987 because of good post play. Daryl Thomas was posted up along the free-throw lane. Keith Smart took an extra dribble to create a good passing lane, and fed Thomas. Daryl was a good post-up player, so Smart's defender instinctively moved down to help guard him. Daryl simply passed the ball back to Smart, who dribbled toward the baseline and hit a routine jump shot for the game-winning basket.*

■■

Also keep in mind the importance of re-posting. If you catch a pass after posting up but are unable to free yourself for a shot, pass the ball back to someone on the perimeter. Your defender probably will relax at this point, enabling you to sit down on his/her thighs, post up again closer to the goal and get a shot.

Most effective offenses utilize inside-out play, meaning the ball is passed to and from post players to make the defense adjust and work harder. Having an effective post player — and it can be a guard — makes this much easier to achieve.

Guards should not overlook post moves. They add to your offensive arsenal and make you a more effective player. Post moves aren't only for big players, they are for players. Period.

SHOOTING

The bottom line in basketball is shooting. No matter how well you execute your offense, no matter how great your skills might be in other areas, no matter how athletic you are, if your team cannot shoot well, it will not be very successful. As long as the outcome of basketball games is determined by which team scores the most points, shooting will be important.

Most guards are shooters first and foremost. They grow up shooting around in the driveway at home, or at the park or schoolyard, and develop shooting skills at an early age. Unfortunately, too many players go about it the wrong way and acquire bad habits that are difficult to overcome.

Shooting should always be practiced at game speed. Don't walk around and throw up shots halfheartedly while talking to friends or daydreaming. Get something out of your practice by shooting as you would in a game. Put your legs into the shot, follow through and shoot off of the move. And practice only the shots you would take in a game. It

isn't necessary to spend hour after hour working on your shot if you use your time efficiently.

Develop good habits

Good habits, in shooting a basketball or anything else, are best developed early because bad habits are difficult to break.

Many players begin shooting without supervision and adopt an unorthodox style. You occasionally find a great shooter with unusual form, but not very often. While there always is room for individual style, all players should conform to certain fundamentals when shooting.

If you are right-handed, the ball should be shot from the right side of your head. Some players release the ball from the opposite side or from in front of their heads, but this means they aren't moving their arms in a straight line as they release the ball.

Your non-shooting hand should not interfere with your stroke. Some players allow the thumb of the non-shooting hand to "participate" in the shot. Use as few body parts as possible when shooting. Just as with a machine, the fewer the number of parts, the better.

If you have a poor release, practice by simply releasing the ball against a wall or into the air with just one hand. Bend your legs and follow through by extending your arm and snapping your wrist as you release the ball. After you have mastered the simple fundamentals you can begin using your non-shooting hand to help control the ball.

If you have bad shooting habits, correcting your fundamentals will be frustrating. You will be tempted to give up and go back to your familiar style because it's more comfortable, and, for the time being, more successful. But this is an investment for the future that will pay off handsomely in the long run. Don't worry about your success as you develop good habits. It will come with time.

Make it a point to get in a certain number of shots per day, and shoot from all areas of the court where you might shoot in a game. Use the backboard when the angle of the shot permits it. Chart your shots so that you can keep track of how many you shoot and how many you hit.

Start by shooting closer shots and concentrating on your form. As you improve and get older, move away from the basket. Don't practice three-pointers until you are consistent from 15 feet.

STEVE: *I finished my college career as Indiana's all-time leading scorer (Calbert Cheaney has since broken my record) and scored about 5,500 points in my high school, college and professional career. But I never dunked the ball, and very few of them came on layups. Probably 80 percent of my points came from jump shots and free throws.*

Get lined up

One of the most overlooked aspects in shooting is catching the ball properly. Most shots in organized play will come off of a pass. Your coach certainly isn't going to want you dribbling around hunting for a shot while your teammates stand and watch.

You need to be able to catch the ball and square up to the basket as smoothly and quickly as possible. If you release the ball with your body at an angle to the basket, your shooting percentage will suffer.

All players should assume triple-threat position after catching the ball. This means they are squared-up and facing the basket putting them in a position to do one of three things when they get the ball: shoot, dribble or pass. The more options you have with the ball, the greater threat you are to the defense.

You can practice this by yourself, if necessary. Throw the ball into the air with backward spin so it bounces back to you. Catch it and get your shooting hand on the middle of the basketball as quickly as possible while squaring up to shoot. Bend your legs, place your shooting foot slightly ahead of your non-shooting foot and have your eyes on the rim. Do this until it comes naturally.

Your shooting foot (the right foot for a right-hander, the left foot for a left-hander) should point toward the basket and be slightly in front of the other foot. If your foot is not pointed correctly you have to alter your form to compensate, which throws off your shot.

The sum total of all this is that you should shoot in a straight line. Your arm follows a straight line toward the basket and your shooting foot is lined up as well. If you do this you reduce your margin for error dramatically because you aren't likely to shoot left or right. You might shoot too short or long, but even then you sometimes get a favorable bounce off the rim or backboard and still score.

See the target

You wouldn't close your eyes before shooting, but many players do the next-worst thing by not focusing on the rim. Although looking at the rim seems like the obvious thing to do when shooting, it's surprising the number of players who don't look at the rim until a split-second before shooting the ball.

Rifle or archery marksmen don't wait until the last moment to look at the target before pulling the trigger or releasing the string. They focus on it for a long time. The speed at which basketball is played doesn't allow you to spend a lot of time staring at the basket, but you still should be able to get a good look at it before releasing the ball.

Focusing on the rim should be part of the process of assuming the triple-threat position. Fix your eyes on the front of the rim. If you are going to shoot a bank shot, focus on the square above the rim.

■■

ED: *When I played in college I was always more interested in getting assists than shots. This hurt me as a shooter because I tended to be looking for an open teammate when I caught the ball. Then if I shot I didn't look at the rim until the last moment before releasing the ball. I had to discipline myself to focus on the rim longer and use my peripheral vision to pass if an opportunity came up.*

■■

Use the proper equipment

Young players should use a ball smaller than regulation size and shoot at a basket lower than 10 feet to help them develop proper fundamentals. A young person trying to shoot a regulation-size ball at a 10-foot basket must strain to get the ball to the rim, probably developing bad habits in the process.

Using equipment appropriate to a player's age enables that boy or girl to have more success, and that will only encourage that player to keep playing. All kids want to have success as quickly as possible, and this will help them do so. The more fun kids have while doing something, the more they want to do it.

Preparing for the shot

If you have good shot preparation you will create shots for yourself, particularly against a zone defense. This includes positioning yourself and catching the ball properly. As you grow older and play at higher levels, you will learn that it is much easier to make shots than it is to get shots.

If you're ready to shoot the ball before it gets to you — hands and feet positioned properly, knees bent, body lined up with the basket — you will be able to get off the shot much more quickly and score, even if your defender is quicker than you are. Use the time that elapses while the pass is coming toward you to prepare for the shot so that all you have to do after catching the ball is pivot into your shot and release the ball — a simple two-step process. The pivot with the inside foot and the planting of the outside foot are extremely important. Do the movement crisply, so that your outside shoe squeaks.

Practice shot preparation by simply having somebody throw passes to you as you cut. Catch the ball with your hands in position to shoot so that you don't have to rotate it before releasing. For a right-handed player, this means catching the ball with your left hand on the side of the ball and the right hand on top of it. Obviously you cannot do this with a poorly thrown pass; with a bad pass, you must concentrate on merely controlling the ball.

Even when you are standing still during a game you should be in a position to shoot. Don't stand straight up with your feet at odd angles. Be prepared to shoot if a pass is thrown to you.

It all comes down to efficiency and eliminating as many steps as possible. Edwin Moses, the great 400-meter hurdler, became the best in the world by eliminating one step between each set of hurdles. While other hurdlers had to take 15 or 14 steps between hurdles, Moses only needed 13. It is much the same with shooting. If you can eliminate as many "steps" as possible in the shooting process, you have a much better chance of getting off your shot.

You will find that you do not need a variety of great moves or an amazing vertical jump to score at higher levels of play. If you know how to prepare for your shot and have the correct form and have a range that includes a three-point shot, you can score.

Finishing the job

Follow-through is the last, but not least, step in the shooting process. Too many players set up and line up properly, but spoil their shot by not executing a simple follow-through correctly.

Your body should be leaning toward the basket slightly, or be straight-up, and the wrist should snap as you release the ball. This is sometimes called a "goose neck" because of the shape your hand and wrist assume after releasing the ball properly.

Hold your follow-through for awhile. Some fans might see this as a cocky gesture, but it really reinforces your effort to follow through properly rather than "pulling the string" and jerking your hand backward after releasing the ball. Show your confidence in your shooting form by holding your follow-through with your hand high in the air as the ball goes through the net.

Be a faker

Using proper form and doing it consistently enables you to fake a shot when necessary to throw off the defense. You do everything just as you would when shooting except release the ball. After the defense reacts you can act accordingly, by either driving by your defender if you have not dribbled or shooting as the defender comes down.

Left: the follow-through should be held after the release of the free throw or jump shot. It is sometimes called the "goose neck."

Everything else should be the same. You're in triple-threat position, your legs are bent, your hands are set properly and you are focused on the rim as you catch the ball. Many young players, if they know they are not going to shoot, do not bend their legs. Then they have to reload and assume the triple-threat stance. By the time they do this the defense might have had time to recover and prevent them from shooting.

Remember, with a shot fake: When the ball goes up, the butt does down. And the ball should be raised high enough that you can see the rim underneath the basketball, or at least get the ball to eye level where you can execute the shot if the defender doesn't react to the fake.

Use the glass

A bank shot is effective from certain angles on the floor, because it gives you a greater margin of error. It has become a lost art. Too many players refuse to use it.

It is important, however, to know before you go up for your shot whether or not you are going to use the backboard. If you are uncertain, you almost certainly will miss. Make it a habit. Either bank the ball off the backboard every time you shoot from an angle, or never bank at all.

■■■

STEVE: *I used to call out "bank" every time I shot off the backboard. Some people might have considered that talking trash, but I did it to reinforce my intention. I wasn't going to second-guess myself. I called it out as I went up for the shot, and followed through with it.*

■■■

Drills

Countless shooting drills are available to make your workout more efficient and more fun.

One is to simply go "around the horn." Start from the baseline and move around the three-point arc after each shot. Shoot 10 shots. Keep track of how many you hit. Continue in a full 180-degree arc around the basket. You might shoot 10 free throws after each set.

When possible, have someone rebound for you so that you can get in more shots in a short amount of time and develop a rhythm. This also will enable you to practice being in proper position when you catch the ball and get off your shot quickly.

You also can work with another player who acts as a defender. That person stands in front of the basket, throws the ball to you and sprints out to try to block the shot. This forces you to catch the ball properly and get off the shot quickly before it is blocked. The two players exchange places and repeat the process. You also can work on a shot fake in the same drill.

conditions. You can incorporate fakes and shooting off the dribble as well. Keep track of how many shots you take and make. It is a good idea to chart them so you can track your improvement.

If possible, do these drills with a partner of similar ability. Assign spots on the court to shoot from and keep track of your score. Incorporate free throws into the mix. Take turns. Talk to each other, tease each other to force each other to concentrate. After all, in a game you'll have to shoot with fans screaming at you trying to distract you.

As with all drills, use your imagination to make your workouts more fun and challenging.

FREE THROWS

Shooting free throws is probably the simplest aspect of the game, yet many players — even in the NBA — do not do it well. In fact, over the past few years, free-throw percentages at the highest levels of play have declined.

Why? Lack of practice and concentration, primarily. There is no excuse for being a poor free-throw shooter because you can always practice more, and you can always concentrate.

Countless games are decided at the foul line; not just in the final seconds, but throughout the game. Just imagine how many more games a team would win during the course of the season if it improved its overall free-throw percentage by just a few points, such as from 65 to 70 percent.

Becoming a good foul shooter, in fact, is a good way to earn more playing time. When a game is close, coaches are reluctant to play poor foul shooters because they can cost their team a victory. You might be slow or lack skills in certain areas, but if you can hit foul shots you'll be an important team member.

Make it routine

The most important thing in shooting foul shots is to establish a routine and do it every time. The basic fundamentals of shooting apply — holding the ball properly, lining up correctly and following through — but you can prepare for your shot any way you like.

You can spin the ball, dribble it a set number of times, wipe your hands a certain way... whatever, do it every time so that it becomes a habit.

■■■

STEVE: *When I was a senior in high school, I scored 57 points against Broad Ripple in the state tournament. The thing I was most proud of, however, was hitting 25 of 25 free throws in that game. In our game later that night against Connersville, who beat us and went on to win the state title, I hit 11 of 11. I wound up hitting all 36 of my free-throw attempts that day.*

I also remember having two foul shots with five seconds left in an important game against Anderson earlier that year. We were down one point, and I missed both of them. I was so upset because I had disciplined myself at the foul line with my imaginary games and I hadn't made the most of that opportunity.

I responded by working harder than ever, and I didn't miss two free throws in a row again until we played UNLV in the semifinals of the NCAA tournament my senior year in college.

Shooting free throws is a simple four-step process.

1. Find the nail hole or spot in the floor at the center of the foul line. These are used by custodians and architects to make proper measurements. Place your shooting foot on the nail hole, this will line up your lower body for the shot.

2. Find the valve stem in the basketball and place your index finger just to the left of it and your middle finger to the right (for a right-hander). This lines up your upper body and enables you to hold the ball the same way every time. If you happen to use a ball with a valve stem on the side of the ball rather than the middle, find another spot, such as a letter, to help you line up the shot.

3. Focus intently on the basket, blocking out all other thoughts and distractions. Look over the front edge of the rim. You will have confidence because you are lined up by following steps one and two.

4. Make the shot. Hitting free throws is an attitude, something to approach with mental intensity. Too many players view them as a break in the game and a chance to rest. They're free points, so take them. Take pride in making the defense take the ball out of bounds after you shoot.

Lining up your shot properly cannot be overemphasized. As with shooting field goals, if you are lined up you reduce by half the possibility of missing the shot. You won't miss left or right, you'll only miss short or long. That alone will improve your shooting percentage dramatically.

Remember Steve's four-step process for foolproof free throw shooting:

1. Nail Hole
2. Ball Hole
3. Basket Hole
4. Take it Out

Make it a point to shoot a minimum number of free throws every day. Most players score at least 20 percent of their points from the foul line. Why not devote close to 20 percent of your practice time to foul shots?

You can challenge yourself by enforcing a standard. Refuse to end your workout until you have hit a certain number of free throws in a row — perhaps five for young players and seven to 10 for older players. Put pressure on yourself to simulate game situations.

You can incorporate conditioning by "penalizing" yourself for each missed free throw. For example, run a sprint or do a certain number of push-ups every time you miss. This helps you learn to cope with pressure during games. If you step up to the line with the score tied and only a few seconds remaining in the game, you want to be accustomed to having dealt with pressure.

It is important to practice free throws between drills or at the end of a workout, because you want to practice when you are tired. Again, when you are shooting important foul shots late in the game, you want to be prepared.

Chart your free throws to track your percentage, and keep the charts so you can measure your progress. We have included examples of our charts at the end of this chapter.

You also can make free-throw shooting a competitive drill with a partner. Instead of playing H-O-R-S-E and throwing up crazy shots, why not shoot free throws in sets of 10 and see who can hit the most? That would be far more constructive and relevant to game situations. Put up a prize for the winner to make it more competitive and fun.

No matter how you decide to go about practicing free throws, make sure you do it. You'll be glad you did after you hit the game-winner.

PASSING

Passing is a crucial skill for all basketball players, particularly guards. Think about it: you pass the ball during a game far more often than you shoot it. And in a well-executed offense, most field goals are set up by a pass. A team cannot efficiently score without good passing.

Yet passing is perhaps the rarest skill in basketball. A lot of players are great shooters and many handle the ball well. But how many great passers can you think of? That's what made Magic Johnson and Larry Bird so unique. They always recognized an open teammate and were able to get the ball to him.

Besides, if you are a great scorer the defense eventually will find a way to take away your shot, even if it has to double- or triple-team you. Any player who draws special emphasis from the defense can be a great asset to his or her team by being able and willing to pass the ball.

All good teams pass the ball well. That doesn't mean they execute fancy no-look passes through the legs of defenders. It just means they constantly look for the open man and know how to execute the fundamental passes.

Most effective offenses get the ball to a post player on a regular basis because it puts more pressure on the defense and makes it easier for perimeter players to get open. But the ball must be passed to the post first. This skill — the post feed — alone is a crucial aspect of basketball.

Setting yourself up

Probably the most common mistake among passers is that they get lazy and do not make crisp passes. A weak pass usually leads to a turnover, often resulting in a layup by the other team.

This cannot be emphasized enough. Most passes intercepted by defenders are not inaccurate, they are too soft. This doesn't mean you throw the ball as hard as you can. Experience and common sense will teach you the proper velocity for a good pass.

As a general rule, throw the ball to the hand away from the defender. This is very basic, but often overlooked. You can eliminate at least two or three turnovers a game by following this simple rule.

To make the proper pass, however, you must have the correct passing angle. As a rule, do not throw a teammate the ball unless you can see the numbers on his or her jersey. Then throw the ball to the hand away from the defense. Most turnovers off of post passes result when the passer cannot see the numbers of the target.

Passing lanes also must be created because in most cases you will not be able to make a simple chest pass. You do this by faking. Fake low to throw high and fake high to throw low. Fake right before making a hook pass to the left. Dribble one way, then reverse and pass with the opposite hand. These moves create openings to make a simple pass.

Post passing is a vital skill for every guard. Fake high to throw low and fake low to throw high are simple rules to get the ball successfully inside.

Fakes also help the player to whom you are passing. If you fake high to a post player, for example, that player's defender might go for the fake and be out of position when the post player catches the ball. That will enable the post player to score more easily.

You can incorporate fakes into your passing skills by faking a pass to a teammate, dribbling the other way, then turning back and passing to that teammate. Good passers keep the defense off balance, just as good pitchers in baseball keep hitters off balance.

The best passing distance is 10 to 15 feet. There are exceptions, of course, such as on fast breaks or when throwing skip passes. But in a half-court offense, most passes will be of medium range.

Obviously, passers must keep their heads up so they can see the court. Many young players, and even some older ones, look at the ball or at the floor while dribbling and fail to see open teammates. If you keep your head up and your eyes focused near the rim you should be able to see the entire floor.

The fundamental passes

The two-handed chest pass is the most basic of all passes. Simply hold the ball with a hand on each side and step into the pass. Snap your palms to put backspin on the ball so that the ball stays on course and is easier to catch.

The bounce pass is often underutilized. The ball should bounce about two-thirds of the way toward the target. Like all passes, it should be executed sharply to reduce the odds it will be intercepted. Bounce passes are often preferred over other passes, particularly when trying to get the ball to a post player. They are often easier to catch. They are almost always preferred on a fast break, because your teammate can adjust his pace and path toward the basket to catch the ball and the defender will have more difficulty getting a hand on the ball.

Keep in mind that a bounce pass delivered from the chest probably will bounce up to the receiver's chest while a bounce pass delivered from the knees will only bounce up to the receiver's knees. Know which is the most appropriate when you make the pass.

All players should master these basic passes before attempting the passes that will put them on the highlight film. Too many young players try to throw passes from behind the back or between the legs before they have learned the more basic skills. Fancy passes by more advanced players have their place but only when a more routine pass will not work.

It is important for players to be able to pass with their "weak" hand. If you are right-handed, you should be able to make a left-handed bounce pass to a post player, for example. If you can't, your offensive options are severely limited.

Also, keep in mind the importance of your fingertips in passing. They release the ball, so it obviously is important that you strengthen them as much as possible.

Becoming a better passer

Aside from understanding the basics of passing — which pass is appropriate for which situation, passing angles, and so on — you improve your passing skills simply by passing.

Whenever you play in a pickup game, whether it is two-on-two, five-on-five full-court or anything in between, concentrate on making good passes and setting up teammates for baskets. You can always work on your shooting when you are alone. Pickup games offer a great opportunity to improve passing and other skills.

Young players should always try to play in pickup games with older players to speed their improvement. This in particular is a great time to work on passing, because older players generally don't want young kids shooting a lot. If you are playing with older and better players, accept your role and concentrate on passing. They'll love playing with you.

A crucial aspect of passing is knowing where all of your teammates are going to be. A quarterback doesn't drop back to pass without knowing where his receivers are supposed to go. In basketball, all of your teammates are potential receivers. A guard should know the team's offense so well that he or she knows where all of his or her teammates are supposed to cut. Then you can anticipate and deliver the ball at the moment they arrive at their destination.

That, more than anything, is what makes great passers great: recognition and anticipation. If you were to talk with less accomplished players who participated in a pickup game with a great passer such as Magic or Bird, they would tell you that they received passes at times when they didn't even realize they were open. Passing a basketball is very simple. The difficult part is knowing exactly when to do it and which pass to use.

You can work on your passing during the most routine moments. If you are shooting around with a few friends and taking turns rebounding for each other, don't just casually return the ball to them. Make a sharp pass and deliver it where they can catch and shoot with no wasted motion.

You also can work on your passing by yourself by passing against a wall or a tossback — an upright frame with a tightly woven net that returns the ball to you. Pick a target and try to deliver crisp passes from all angles while stationary and on the move.

This is an excellent time to practice riskier passes. You won't embarrass yourself or take the chance of being pulled from the game if your no-look pass misses your target on the wall.

People play pitch-and-catch all the time with a baseball. Why not do it in basketball, too? Start by standing 10 or 15 feet from your partner and pass the ball back and forth, making all the potential passes. Then do it while on the move. This can be done with anyone, including your mother and father. If you are practicing with another player, work up to where both of you are moving, as in a game situation.

A simple way to improve passing skills is with a game of keep-away. Two players can stand about 15 feet apart with a defender in the middle, or three or more players can stand in a triangle or circle around a defender. The passers try to get the ball to one another despite the defender's efforts to intercept or deflect the ball. Obviously, they will need to use fakes and a variety of passes to accomplish this.

If possible, use more than one ball in a passing drill. Two players can pass to each other (without a defender) simultaneously while making different passes. One player throws a bounce pass while the other throws a chest pass or overhead pass, for example.

Do it often, do it well

Passing becomes easier as you become more familiar with your teammates and how they like to play. If you know what they like to do and what they can do, you can make better decisions during games. You obviously don't want to pass to a poor ball handler running the court if you also can hit another guard with better skills. The same is true in your half-court offense. It doesn't do much good to pass the ball to someone who is not in position to do anything with the ball.

When trapped, take the trap low, step wide and look to pass by the defender's thigh.

Know where the scorers like to receive the ball. If the best shooter on your team prefers a chest pass rather than a bounce pass, keep that in mind — likewise if your post players prefer bounce passes over chest passes.

Do not make the mistake of believing you have to make great passes to get a lot of assists. Watch a game sometime and focus on the passes the guards make. The vast majority are routine passes that are made quickly before the defense has time to react.

The best offenses are those in which the ball is passed quickly and often, and quick decisions are essential to making quick passes. If you know where you are going to pass the ball before it even gets to you, you have a great advantage over the defense. Or if you are dribbling the ball and can spot an opening immediately, you should be able to make the pass and beat the defense. Don't "tease" the defense by standing with the ball and faking all over the place. This tends to grind your offense to a halt and also gives the defense an opportunity to double-team you.

If you get trapped often during games, this is an indication you are not moving well or making quick decisions and passes. When you do get trapped, however, such as when the defense is pressing full-court, you should take the trap low, move your non-pivot foot to step wide and around the defender and look for an open teammate. Use fakes if necessary.

Again, you do not need to make fancy passes to be an effective passer. The more often you attempt behind-the-back passes or passes through heavy traffic, the more likely you are to make turnovers — and turnovers are always one of the biggest factors in whether your team wins or loses.

Guards should take pride in their assist-to-turnover ratio. At higher levels, coaches look for a ratio of at least three-to-one — such as six assists and two turnovers. Treat the ball like it's made of solid gold. Take care of it as if you will lose it forever if you throw it away just once. You can help yourself in this area by keeping things basic.

Keep in mind that in basketball, as in life, the more you give the more you get. The more passes you make to teammates, the more you will receive from them. Nobody likes to play with a selfish player who tries to control the ball all of the time. Passing is an unselfish act that should make you feel good, just like doing a favor for someone off the court.

■■

STEVE: *One of my great memories of high school basketball is the last home game of my career. My dad put my younger brother into the game toward the end so that we could play together one time. We were running an out-of-bounds play. He came off a screen, I inbounded to him and he hit a jump shot. Of all the assists in my career, that's the one I remember most.*

■■

DEFENSE

About half of your time in each game is spent on defense. But do you devote half of your practice time to defense? It's doubtful anybody does.

Defense isn't as fun or as glamorous as offense. They rarely show defensive highlights on television unless someone makes a great steal that leads to a basket or blocks a shot. But great defenders get playing time. All successful teams play good defense, and a great defender is an important ingredient. A poor defender, meanwhile, makes it difficult for the coach to play him or her. Even great scorers might have to leave the game if they do not defend well. And if you aren't in the game, you can't make the game-winning shot or other plays that people will remember.

Athleticism is more important on defense than offense. A player with good size, quick feet and long arms has a great advantage defensively. But a less athletic player can become a good defender by following certain fundamentals and principles — as long as that player is in top condition.

One of the most important aspects of playing defense is anticipation. If you are a good offensive player you probably can anticipate offensive movement. This translates to defense, too. Imagine how much more successful you will be as a defender, for example, if you can anticipate a pass and step into the passing lane.

Coaches have different approaches to defense regarding double-teaming and helping out away from the ball. Some even want to play zone. But defense starts with your ability to guard an opponent one-on-one. This is why playing someone one-on-one is so valuable. Not only do you improve your ballhandling and shooting skills, you improve your defense. Place just as much emphasis on your defense when playing a pickup game, no matter how many players are involved.

Self-confidence is as important defensively as it is on offense. You must believe you can stop your opponent and attack your job aggressively. Concentrate on your footwork and your stance, and challenge yourself to stop your opponent. When you play in a pickup game, try to guard the other team's best player, and try to guard people full-court whenever possible. Challenge yourself.

That doesn't mean taking unnecessary risks, however. If you gamble too much and go for steals all the time, you take yourself out of position. Experience is the best teacher in learning when to gamble.

The front line of defense

Defense starts with the guards. The inside players have a big responsibility to keep opponents from getting easy baskets, but guards set the tone. If they can keep the players they guard from easily penetrating, and — better yet — if they can create turnovers, they can shut down an offense before it gets started. You'll also find that inside players tend to work harder on defense when the guards are working as hard as possible. Defense is another area in which guards can show leadership.

Teams should take pride in making offensive players turn away from their basket in the halfcourt to protect the ball because of the defensive pressure they face. Keep track of them. The more the better, because if an offensive player isn't facing his or her own basket, that player is in trouble.

Keep this in mind while playing one-on-one: Try to make your opponent turn away from the basket on the perimeter. Nobody can score turned away from the basket unless he or she is close to it.

Many skilled offensive players are like aspirin in water when they face great defensive pressure — they dissolve. When they have to deal with a hustling defender every trip downcourt, they sometimes crack under the pressure. They miss a few shots, or perhaps can't even get shots, and after awhile they stop playing as hard and take themselves out of the offense.

If keeping your opponent from scoring isn't motivation enough, keep this in mind: defense leads to offense. If you are a great defender you'll get a lot of steals, and if that happens you'll get a lot of layups or easy baskets in transition.

Offensive players have enough to worry about without having to worry about the person guarding them. Make them worry about you.

Taking a stance

Stance is the single-most important aspect of playing defense. You cannot stand straight up and guard anyone. You must be wide and low, with your legs spread, knees bent,

Defensive stance is everything! The butt should be down, back straight and hands active to help make you the best defender your physical ability will allow you to be.

butt down, back straight and arms active. One basic rule is that your head should be below your opponent's shoulders.

As players get tired, they tend to come out of their stance and stand up straighter. Be conscious of this and fight it. Make sure your legs — particularly your thighs — are in shape so that you can play good defense for long stretches of time.

Learn to be comfortable in a defensive stance. Do this by getting in shape and getting used to moving quickly without standing up. If a good offensive player sees you standing upright, that player is going to take advantage by driving right by you for an assist or easy basket.

Footwork also is a vital element of defense. Move your feet constantly while staying on your toes. You might not be as quick as the player you are guarding, but you can neutralize him through sheer effort, positioning and conditioning.

The most basic rule of one-on-one defense is that you do not cross your feet while playing in the halfcourt. Take short, choppy steps, with your foot pointed slightly in the direction you are moving. Stay wide, however; if your feet get too close together your opponent will be able to blow by you.

The proper movement in the defensive stance is a push-and-reach motion. When moving to your left, for example, push off your right foot and reach with your left. Push and reach, push and reach.

It is important to keep your arms active because they enable you to move more quickly. Keeping your arms active makes you seem more athletic. The opponent will be more concerned with keeping the ball away from your active arms and less concerned with driving by you or shooting over you. If your hands are still, you pose no threat to the player with the ball.

Be offensive when on defense

When playing defense you are attempting to take away the angle of your opponent. You want to keep that player from cutting to the basket or into an open space on the floor. That usually means keeping the opponent away from the middle of the floor and trying to force that player toward the baseline or sideline.

This is particularly important for guards because a guard who passes and handles the ball well can do a lot of damage from the middle of the floor. From there, he or she can do almost anything.

Fakes are important defensively as well as offensively. After you learn to anticipate an offensive player's movement you can keep that player off balance by faking a steal or faking as if you are going to fall for a shot fake.

As a defender, you should be a predator, not the prey. Be offensive even when you are on defense. Dominate your opponent regardless of which end of the floor you are playing.

Right: Ed shows an excellent contest of Steve's shot. Notice how Ed's hand is extended and how the body is turning in the air to prevent a body foul and setting up his block out.

Left: Ed blocks out the shooter. His hands are up and his butt is on the offensive player's thighs.

One aspect of this approach is to contest every shot taken. Even if you are too far from your opponent to block the shot, have your hand up and jump at his or her shot. Shout "shot!" to distract the shooter and warn your teammates that they need to get into rebounding position. Watch a game sometime and check the percentage of contested shots that are missed as opposed to uncontested shots. The difference is staggering.

You don't want to jump unnecessarily, however. Your opponent probably will be trying to get you to leave your feet so he or she can get you off balance. Don't leave your feet until the player you are guarding jumps. When you jump, have your legs spread and turn in the air. This not only helps you avoid a foul but also enables you to assume a box-out position after the shot is taken.

Just as shooters must follow through, defenders must do the same. On defense, the rebound is the ultimate follow-through. After you box out, go after the ball. There is no reason guards cannot be effective rebounders because many missed shots deflect out to the perimeter where the guards are likely to be positioned.

Aggressive defenders will want to try to steal the ball. This is great, but they must know when to pick their spots. If you go for a steal and fail, you give the ball handler an opening to the basket. It will be difficult to ever steal the ball from a good ball handler, so it is important to play it safe most of the time and concentrate on positioning.

At times, however, opportunities for a steal present themselves. Set up the ball handler with fakes. Fake at the ball over and over without lunging for it to keep the ball handler off balance. After awhile that player will become comfortable in the belief you will not really try to steal the ball. That's when you have your best opportunity to go for it.

The best time to go for a steal from a ball handler is when he or she is not touching the ball. This means you should make you move at the moment the ball leaves the hand on its downward flight toward the floor. This gives you the longest amount of time to try to get a hand on the ball — all of the downward flight and all of the upward bounce until the ball handler touches it again.

You can study the dribbler's motions to gauge the precise moment the ball leaves his hand. You might want to say "now" to yourself or out loud every time the ball begins its downward flight so you become familiar with the rhythm. After awhile you'll know the precise moment to spring for the ball.

Positioning

The best way to control your opponent defensively is through proper positioning. Be aggressive and get after your opponent, but you do not want to take unnecessary risks, either. It takes experience to know when to go for a steal. Most of the time you want to stay between your opponent and the basket.

If you are guarding a player with the ball your belly button should be on that player's inside hip. In other words, if you were to draw a line from the player's hip to the basket, the line would run through your midsection. You can control your player this way, because there is only one direction the player can go, and you know which way that is — away from the middle of the court.

The bottom line of defense on the ball is to not get beat. You don't want your opponent to get by you for an easy shot or pass. If you do, the offense suddenly has a numerical advantage — five-on-four at the least — and will have less trouble scoring.

Watch a game and you will see that most baskets are scored because an individual got beat — if not off the dribble, away from the ball. When this happens, defensive chaos results because a teammate has to help you, and someone else has to cover for your teammate. Assume the responsibility of not getting beat.

Guarding a great scorer

You are not likely to shut out a great scorer. Your objective is to make life as difficult as possible for that player throughout the game.

The foremost objective is to keep the ball out of that player's hands. Nobody can score without the ball, so you want to emphasize your defensive efforts away from the ball. Your effort alone might wear down the scorer and break his or her will. Many scorers do not move well without the ball, so you have a better chance to stop them before they get the ball rather than after.

If you are in better physical condition than your opponent, he or she might not have the strength to score late in the game if you have made that player work hard throughout. Make the player cut and get to the ball a couple more times than usual to get off a shot. Over the course of a game this adds up to a lot of effort and might prevent the scorer from getting off good shots or being able to make good shots as the game progresses.

Another aspect of controlling scorers is keeping them from getting comfortable. You do this by mixing up your defensive approach. Guard them a little differently each time. Try to block their path while cutting one time, simply maintain good position the next time. Play them tightly one time, give them a step the next time (but keep your hands up). Don't talk trash, but talk. Shout as they take a shot.

If they have a favorite spot on the floor from which to shoot, don't let them get to that spot — and if they do, don't let them shoot from there. If a player isn't effective dribbling to the left, position yourself so that is the only direction available to him or her.

You can contest the shot in different ways, too. Fly at them with a hand in their face and shout one time. Another time you might fly by them and head downcourt to try to get a layup.

Make that player work hard when he or she is on defense, too. Many great scorers don't like to work hard on defense, so take advantage of this. Cut hard and make them move a lot to keep you from getting easy shots. Sprint downcourt in transition. It's often a battle of wills.

It's a mental game, too. At the high school or collegiate level, you should be able to get a video tape of the opponent's game. Study the game so you know what that player likes to do — then try to prevent it. Where do they like to shoot? Do they prefer to shoot off the dribble or off a pass? Can they go to their weak side? Is a player susceptible to charging if you position yourself properly? Know these things and you'll be much more successful.

Defense off the ball

Defense doesn't stop when your man does not have the ball. You must continue your defensive effort and principles away from the ball. As mentioned earlier, most baskets come off of passes, not dribbling. Don't be susceptible to a pass that sets up an easy basket. Maintain your stance, your balance and your concentration.

Steve taking away the flash post by beating the offensive player to the spot.

Close out: Ed sprints to get to the shooter (above). He then chops the last two or three steps with the hand up to get his body under control and to keep the ball in front of the defense (below).

On the other hand, if you can maintain good defense away from the ball and prevent your opponent from getting passes, that player is likely to stop playing as hard — which makes your job much easier.

One aspect of defense away from the ball is preventing your opponent from flashing to accept a pass in scoring position. You do this by staying between your man and the ball and extending the elbow closest to the player you are guarding to block his or her path. This is commonly called taking away the flash post.

If the player is cutting away from you to receive a pass, play good denial defense. You keep the hand closest to that player near his or her midsection and your outside hand raised in a denial position with the palm facing the ball so you can deflect a pass. Be in the proper stance and slide your feet aggressively to be able to get to the ball.

If you get beat for a moment, such as on a backcut, turn and open up toward the ball so you can see it and then slide quickly into position. You still must be able to feel your defender, however, and you must maintain a good stance.

You also can snap your head and reverse your direction. You lose sight of the ball for a split-second, which is undesirable, but you might be able to reverse your direction more quickly because you do not leave your basic stance.

Some coaches believe you should open up whenever the player you are guarding reaches the lane so you can see the ball better and try to prevent a post feed. It is more crucial than ever not to take your eyes off the ball when the player you are guarding is close to the basket.

Closing out

A crucial aspect of playing defense is attacking your opponent when he or she takes a pass. There will be times when you are helping a teammate defensively and your assigned player gets the ball.

You must be able to rush toward that player without making yourself vulnerable. If you don't get there quickly enough, you give up an easy jump shot. If you rush out of control, you are prone to fouling or giving up a drive to the basket.

You must move toward your opponent as soon as you see light between the passer's hand and the ball. If you wait too long you won't get to the player receiving the pass in time. Just as with a sprinter in a track meet, it is vital that you get out of the blocks quickly toward your destination.

This small detail can neutralize athleticism. You might not be the quickest player on the floor, but if you get a good jump on your movements that won't be as important. Mental quickness can make up for a lack of physical quickness.

As soon as you are sure the ball is being passed to your opponent, sprint about two-thirds of the way to that player. Then take short, choppy steps in a crouched position with at least one hand held above your head. This enables you to contest a shot and prevent the player with the ball from driving by you. This is commonly called a close-out.

After you reach your assigned player, normal defensive principles apply. Maintain the proper stance and position and force the ball handler away from the middle of the floor.

Slipping the screen or trailing

Staying with the player you are guarding through a screen is one of the most difficult things for a defensive player to do, but it's one of the most powerful methods of neutralizing an offense. Good offenses take advantage of many screens, and the defense must be able to cope with them.

If you are screened by a defender, stay between the player you are guarding and the screener, if possible. Take the arm nearest the screener and use a swim technique, reaching out and around the screener while sliding the leg nearest the screener in a similar motion — out and around. Your armpit should rub the screener so that you remain as narrow as possible. After you slip through the screen, resume the normal defensive position, whether it is on the ball or denial.

This is another reason you should keep your arms active and neither too high or too low. You will be able to feel the screener as you move past him and execute the proper swim technique to slip by him.

Another way to defend a player running off of a screen is to trail him or her. Simply get right behind your man and follow behind tightly. This forces the player to make a tight or curl cut. This also makes the offensive player make plays in traffic.

Talk the talk

Communication is essential for all defensive players because you must help each other. You and your teammates must tell each other when a screen is coming or where the player they are guarding is headed. Shout "screen left!" or "screen right!"

The inside defenders in particular must communicate as much as possible because they can see the floor the best. As a guard, you often have your back to the rest of the floor, so you have to rely on the verbal help of inside players. Keep reminding them to do it — and do the same for them as often as possible.

Talking is contagious on defense, even if it is idle chatter at times. This helps keep everyone's enthusiasm high and offers another distraction to the offensive team. If your defensive pressure is not enough to distract them, perhaps they'll be distracted by your conversation.

Talking is particularly effective at higher levels when teams have scouted their opponents and know what they want to do offensively. If you know where an opposing player is supposed to cut you can shout out a warning to a teammate.

In the photo above, Steve shows ball-you-man defensive position. Notice that he points to both the ball and his man.

For example, if your assigned player is setting a backscreen, you can shout "backscreen!" to your teammate who is being picked to warn him so he can position himself accordingly. It's deflating to an offense to think you're always one step ahead.

Talk! It makes defense more fun.

Condition yourself

Conditioning obviously is important for defenders, and one of the best methods of staying in shape and improving footwork at the same time is jumping rope.

This used to be the most common form of exercise for athletes who rely on footwork — not only basketball players, but boxers and others as well. It has become something of a lost art, but you should make it a regular part of your workout. It improves footwork, coordination and aerobic conditioning all at once.

Be a visionary

Just as offensive players must see as much of the floor as possible, defenders must do the same. You must be able to see picks being set, cutters moving away from the ball and everything else that is developing so that you can react accordingly or shout help to a teammate.

The ball-you-man theory is one of the basic defensive principles, and it relies on good vision. You always want to stay between the ball and your defensive assignment when you are away from the ball. You can only do this by keeping your head up and using your peripheral vision to see the man and the ball. It is also called midpointing, because you look at a point between the man and the ball to see both.

Drills

All defensive drills involve the proper stance. Even standing in a stance for as long as possible will benefit you by strengthening your leg muscles and helping you to be comfortable in the position.

Add movement by sliding back and forth across the foul lane as quickly as possible and touching each line with your hand. You can even do a drill such as this in your garage or basement. You might think you look silly doing this by yourself, but not as silly as you'll look sitting on the bench because you're a poor defender.

See how long you can go while standing or moving in a defensive stance. Dive on the floor now and then for an imaginary loose ball, then get up and resume your stance. Pound your feet. Slide. Close out. Jump, then touch the floor as you land. Do all the things you have to do on defense.

You can practice sliding in a defensive stance almost anywhere. On the court, slide along the baselines and sidelines, around cones, almost anywhere. Make a track of some sort. Time yourself if you like and keep track of your record. You can also do this in your driveway by placing rocks or almost any object and sliding around them.

Simulate full-court pressure by sliding a few steps laterally, turning and sprinting a few steps, sliding, sprinting and so on. Keep your head at the same level at all times.

It is a good idea to perform some of your drills with your hands behind your back. This forces you to move your feet, which is the most important aspect of playing defense. Later, when you can use your hands, it will seem much easier. You might even want to play defense with your hands behind your back at times during pickup games to focus on your footwork.

Taking charges is another important aspect of defense, and you can work on this with drills as well. For example, zig-zag backward in a defensive stance for half the length of the court, then simulate taking a charge — or, if you are working against an opponent, you can actually take one. Then pop back up as quickly as possible and resume your defense. What if you try to take a charge during a game and it isn't called? You can't sit on the floor and complain, you have to get up as quickly as possible and go find your man.

You can perform drills in a sense while playing in pickup games. For example, focus on a specific aspect of defense, such as not allowing the player you are guarding to shoot without having to dribble first. Or make that player go left. Or keep that player out of the lane. Or slip every screen. As with other skills, some creativity can help you improve and make your work more fun.

So much of defense is developing a quick burst of speed for a few steps. This is how you cut off a player from taking the baseline or driving by you. You do this with drills and conditioning.

■■

STEVE: *As with any skill in basketball, you improve by playing against bigger and older players. If you have an older brother or sister or know an older player, challenge the player one-on-one and try to stop him or her. When I was in fourth grade my dad coached Jerry Sichting, who went on to play at Purdue and in the NBA. I used to bug him all the time, wanting to go one-on-one with him or play H-O-R-S-E. He used to get so aggravated he would lock me in a locker. But it really helped to compete against a player so much better than I was.*

■■

"Who said you can't jump higher, run faster and be more explosive?"

Everybody wants to jump higher, run faster and be more explosive, but not many individuals are willing to pay the necessary price to create the desired improvements in these areas. The following drills will show improvement if they are done two or three times a week over a two-month period for approximately 20 minutes a session. They work!

All of these drills are done in 10-second bursts, because generally, basketball is played in 10-second or less bursts.

1. Jump Rope Simulation — 10 seconds each, 3 sets as fast as you jump
    a. 2-foot jump — feet shoulder-width apart
    b. Right leg only
    c. Left leg only
    d. Jumping jack (legs move as if doing jumping jacks)
    e. Wide base — feet as wide as possible (stay wide)
    f. Split legs forward and back (switch as quickly as you can)

2. Line Jumps — 10 seconds each, 3 sets. Keep hands above ears
    a. Forward and back split — one foot over line, other foot behind line then switch repeatedly
    b. Side of foot next to line — jump back and forth
    c. Switch over top and behind
    d. Straddle — left leg on top, right leg behind, jump over line
    e. Straddle — right leg on top (same as d)

3. Explosion Jumps — 8 jumps of each, 3 sets. Keep hands above ears
    a. Double leg tuck jumps — jump up and bring knees to chest, land and immediately jump up again — repeat
    b. Glute kicks — jump up and bring heels to butt, land, repeat
    c. Lateral jumps — jump as far as you can side to side, land on both feet, immediately jump back laterally, repeat

d. Forward and back — jump forward as far as you can, then backward, repeat

e. Single leg tuck jumps — hold right leg at a right angle, jump up and bring left leg to chest. Keep right leg at right angle, it does not move, repeat

f. Single leg tuck jumps — hold left leg at right angle, bring right leg to chest, repeat

g. Split jumps — right leg forward, left leg back, jump up and bring knees to chest, switch legs so that left leg is forward and right leg is back on landing, repeat

4. Partner Jumps — partner gently puts hands on shoulders of jumper

a. Two feet — jump as high as possible, repeat 10 times

b. One leg — 10 jumps

c. Other leg — 10 jumps

5. Across Court — length of basketball court. Keep hands above ears

a. Repeat standing broad jumps — jump off 2 feet, land, jump as quickly as possible, down the court

b. Lateral jumps — shoulder points to end of court, jump sideways, land on both feet, repeat

c. Lateral jumps — point other shoulder to end of court, jump sideways, land on both feet, repeat

d. Double leg zig-zag — both feet together, jump in zig-zag the length of the court

e. Single leg zig-zag — same as d, but jump on right leg only

f. Single leg zig-zag — other foot

g. Repeated double leg split jump down court

h. Repeated single leg tuck jump down court

i. Repeated single leg tuck jump down court, other leg

j. Power skips — skip with maximum height, jump the length of the court

6. Upper Body — quick workout

a. Do one push-up, go to knees and do one shoulder press

b. Do 2 push-ups, go to knees and do 2 shoulder presses, etc.

c. Repeat until you can't do anymore — a good goal is to build up to 15

These drills should be done on a soft surface like a gym floor or grassy area, so as to lessen the shock on knees. Also, never do these drills two days in a row — always take at least one day off after this workout. These drills will make you better if done over time. Good luck!

SAMPLE WORKOUT I

Purpose of Individual Workout

1. Skill Development
   - A workout that utilizes all phases of enhancing your skill
     - ❏ Ball Handling
     - ❏ Shooting
     - ❏ Footwork
     - ❏ Endurance (Conditioning)
   - A workout that is based on quality of time not quantity of time
   - You are the judge of how hard you work (Intensity level)
   - A workout that, if done with the right intensity will enhance strength and conditioning

What are the Benefits of an Individual Workout?

1. Improved free throw shooting
2. Improvement of basketball skills
3. Conditioning and endurance will improve
4. Development of individual discipline without a coach
5. Confidence improves as skill improves

SAMPLE WORKOUT I (CONTINUED)

Shooting without Dribble (12 to 15 shots)

10 Free Throws

Shooting with Dribble (12 to 15 shots)

10 Free Throws

Bank Shots (10 to 15 shots)

10 Free Throws

Ballhandling 2 Balls and Lines (2 to 4 minutes)

10 Free Throws

Point Moves / Post Moves (12 to 15 shots)

10 Free Throws

Three-point Shots (10 to 12 shots)

10 Free throws

Movement without the Ball (8 to 12 shots)

10 Free Throws

Ballhandling / Attack Dribble and Control (2 to 4 minutes)

10 Free Throws

Rope, Jump Lines, Slides, Backboard Taps (4 to 5 minutes)

10 Free Throws

Repeat Worst Drill of Workout

10 Free Throws

SAMPLE WORKOUT II

Mikan Drill   *(5 minutes)*

Make 20 (10L-10R) hooks

Make 20 (10L-10R) reverses

Make 20 miscellaneous shots and fakes, etc.

Make 5 free throws — record number taken to make five

Ball Handling   *(10 minutes)*

Zig-Zag — use crossover, behind back, between legs, reverse. (2 laps)

Chill Drill — 3 times each side

Kill the Grass — 2 sets, 1 minute each set

Two-up, two-back — 2 sets, 1 minute each set

Make 5 free throws — record number taken to make five

Post Moves   *(10 minutes)*

Execute specific post moves, going block to block, score 10 times (5 each side)

Two sets — using different move each set

Make 5 free throws — record number taken to make five

Shooting   *(30 minutes)*

15 shots — form shooting — 5-10 feet out

Make 5 free throws — record number taken to make five

Make 20 shots — catch, square-up, shoot, record number taken to make 20

Make 10 free throws —record number taken to make 10

Shot fake, 1 dribble — make 20 shots, record number taken to make 20

Make 10 free throws — record number taken to make 10

Shot Fake, 1 dribble — make 20 shots, record number taken to make 20

Make 10 free throws — record number taken to make 10

Fake left, go right, 1 dribble — make 20 shots, record number taken to make 20

Make 10 free throws — record number taken to make 10

Fake right, go left, 1 dribble — make 20 shots, record number taken to make 20

Make 10 free throws — record number taken to make 10

1-on-1 move, pull-up jump shot — make 20 shots, record number taken to make 20

Make 10 free throws — record number taken to make 10

1-on-1 move, layup — make 20 shots, record number taken to make 20

Make 10 free throws — record number taken to make 10

Date Practiced:									
Mikan Drill									
Hooks									
Reverse									
Miscellaneous									
Ball Handling (choose 2) *(check skills done)*									
Zig-zag									
Chill Drill									
Kill the Grass									
Two-up, Two-back									
Post Moves *(check skills done)*									
Drop Step, Base									
Drop Step, Middle									
Fake Middle, Drop Base									
Fake Base, Drop Middle									
Quick Spin									
Sikma									
Shooting *(Record number of shots attempted)*									
Form Shots									
Catch, Square, Shoot									
Shot Fake, One Dribble									
Fake Left, Go Right, One Dribble									
Fake Right, Go Left, One Dribble									
One-on-One Move, Pull-up Jumper									
One-on-One Move, Layup									
120 shots made									
Total number of shots attempted:									
Free throws *(Record number of shots attempted)*									
Five									
Five									
Five									
Five									
Ten									
Ten									
Ten									
Ten									
Ten									
Ten									
80 shots made									
Total number of shots attempted:									

Work out Record Sheet

CONCLUSION

Coaches want to win. That sounds obvious, but players must keep that in mind. Being a nice person isn't enough to win if another player is simply better than you are.

Certainly your attitude and work ethic will influence your playing time, if for no other reason than those attributes will make you a better player. But no coach is going to intentionally lose a game just to play a kid he or she likes.

Athletes should try to put themselves in a position to show they are better than another player. During preseason tryouts, figure out who you have to beat out to make the team and try to go up against that player in drills and scrimmages as often as possible.

The opportunities to improve yourself are endless. Each day contains 24 hours, and you only need about eight to sleep and no more than another eight to go to school or work. What about the remaining hours? If you're trying to become a better player, why can't you get up at 6 a.m. and work out for a couple of hours before school? If it's cold, so what? Dress appropriately. If there's snow on the driveway, grab a shovel. If it's hot, take a water bottle. If there's a way, you can provide the will.

The importance of setting goals has already been discussed, but keep in mind the sacrifices you have to make to meet those goals. One of them is loneliness. Your friends might make fun of you for not going out with them and messing around, but the right thing to do is set a goal and work toward it. You might not always meet your goals, but you'll still accomplish a lot in the process.

When you dedicate yourself to a goal and turn your back on your buddies when they want to goof off, it can be difficult. But you'll also meet other people, more successful people, who are willing to help you. Basketball can bring you into contact with people who will be a positive influence.

Difficult times only make you stronger. You'll learn not to be bothered when certain people don't accept you, because you realize you're doing something positive for yourself. You'll learn what can happen when you set a goal and work toward it. It is worth it!

■■■

ED: *When I was a freshman in high school, I was 5-foot-7 and weighed about 120 pounds. But I loved watching the NCAA tournament, and I set a goal of playing in it someday. I decided I was going to do whatever it took to make it happen. My father, who had been a Division I college player himself, thought I was spending too much time with basketball. It was ironic, because most parents think their kids don't work hard enough.*

On Friday and Saturday nights I would have the spotlight hooked up in the driveway and I would be working on my game. I had an eight-track tape player, and I listened to music while I played. We lived on a busy street, and a lot of cars would be driving by while I was throwing the ball against a toss-back net, passing and cutting, recording my shots.

One time on a Friday night a carload of my buddies drove by. They were buddies, not friends, because your friends care about you and want you to achieve your goals. They don't want to pull you down. These guys came by, stopped and yelled, "Don't you have anything better to do on a Friday night?" I said no, not really. They laughed and called me a few names, threw a few beer bottles and shattered them in the driveway, then took off and sent the gravel in the driveway flying. I can still hear the noise of the bottles crashing and the car taking off. I had tears in my eyes, but that just made me want to work harder.

Four years later I experienced a similar jolt. Instead of beer bottles crashing in the driveway it was the sound of a voice over the public address system. "Welcome, ladies and gentlemen, to today's first-round action in the NCAA basketball tournament. Our first game will be the Miami Redskins against the Maryland Terrapins. Starting at one guard for Miami, 6-foot-1, from Lebanon, Indiana, Ed Schilling."

That sudden disruption was similar to the disruption of the beer bottles breaking in my driveway. It was four years from one to the other, and I'll never forget either one. There I was, playing in the NCAA Tournament against Len Bias and other players I had read about. I was a freshman playing in front of 17,000 people, participating in March Madness.

After that season I was back in that town and ran into some of those same guys who had thrown the beer bottles. They came up and said, "Boy, I saw you on TV. It was great to see one of our boys making it. We were pulling for you." The only difference between me and them was that I had made better use of my time and worked harder at a goal.

STEVE: *When I was in fifth grade I lived in Martinsville, which was a hotbed for basketball. My dad was offered the job at New Castle, which had the largest high school gymnasium in the country, seating about 10,000 people. I didn't really want to leave Martinsville, but the first thing Dad did was take me to the gym at New Castle. I fell in love with it right away. I asked*

Dad if the gym had ever been filled before. He said it hadn't in quite awhile. I said, "When I get in high school, that thing's going to be full."

After my workouts in the gym while I was coming up through high school, I used to sit in the bleachers and look at the arena and try to envision every seat being full and all the lights being turned on. I imagined what it would look like and made it a point to remember that while I worked out.

During the winter, if I couldn't get to the gym, I would shovel the snow off the driveway and play. One of our neighbors would come out and start asking me questions, because he thought there was something wrong with me. "Why are you doing this? What's wrong with you?" We joke about it now. Now he knows why I did it.

■■■

A DAY IN THE LIFE ...

■■■

ED: *When I was in high school, the coach had open gym in the summer. Coach Jim Rosenstihl set the time at 7 a.m., because he knew only the serious players would come that early.*

As the point guard, I thought it was my duty to make sure everyone was there. I had a phone list and went down it every morning at about 6:30 to make sure everyone was up. We usually had our top seven or eight guys at the gym, and we normally had a total of ten to twelve players.

That was one of the keys to our becoming a good team. We didn't have a starter taller than 6-foot-2, yet we went 21-4 and came within one game of reaching the final four of the state tournament. It all went back to those early-morning games in the summer, when we played together for about 90 minutes.

I would stay for another hour or so after those games to work out by myself, then I'd go home and cut the grass or do whatever I needed to do. Then it was time for lunch, and after that I'd go to the park at high noon. That's when I would play with Rick Mount. He'd come by and pick me up, or I would meet him there, and we'd go full-court one-on-one.

We knew nobody else would be crazy enough to be there and we would have the court to ourselves. You can only imagine the comments we would hear. Here's one guy who was out of pro basketball by then, and another little high school kid. We're going full-court, defending each other all over the court and getting after it.

I didn't win a game for two years because he was so much better than me. But after a couple of years I would win a game occasionally. By the time I got in college I could win a series from him occasionally.

We'd play for an hour or 90 minutes. Then we'd sit down or drive around town and he would tell me stories about his playing career, and I'd just eat it up.

Then I'd go home and do some more chores, visit my girlfriend perhaps, get something to eat, and then I'd head back to the park. I'd dribble my ball all the way and try to be the first person there to get some shots in. Then we'd play for two hours full-court, really go at it. The high school team members would stick together. If we lost, we sat down together.

After that I went home and spent time with my parents or friends. There was still time to relax and goof off. But that was a typical day, Monday through Thursday. On the weekend we still played at the park, but maybe there weren't as many people around. I still did my individual workouts, though.

People thought I was nuts. They called me names like Basketball Jones. Sometimes it was condescending, but some of them admired me for it.

It was important to me, just like coaching is important to me now. Those were typical days for me, and they were some of the best days of my life.

STEVE: *A player with average talent who works hard is always going to become better than a player with natural talent who doesn't work hard. I always tried to keep that in mind.*

I remember days that were rainy or just kind of gloomy and I'd think maybe I didn't want to go work out. But then something would get in my mind. I would think, I bet it's clear in another town, and somebody there is working out. So I'd get my rain gear on and head for the gym.

I believe the best workouts I had were on those days, when I thought about not doing it, because you concentrate harder and push yourself harder. There was nothing better than listening to the rain hit the fieldhouse and I knew everyone else in town was inside watching TV or whatever and there I was busting my tail. It was just awesome.

It was a lot of fun too. I always had fun playing basketball. I had a lot of fun playing basketball in my driveway with my boots on. I had a lot of fun drawing up plays on the sidewalk with other kids in the neighborhood when I was little. That's what the game is all about.

It's frustrating as a coach when you can't get your kids to experience the same things you experienced. And there's no reason why they can't if they're willing to pay the price.

ED: *I would write down how many shots I hit from each spot on the floor out of 25 shots. I'd shoot 25 from each baseline, from the angle where I would bank them in, from the top of the key. Then I'd work on one-on-one moves.*

Left: Ed and Steve showing what they did best. Ed is dribbling and Steve is shooting.

I couldn't wait to get home and figure out my percentages. The pages would be all wrinkly and spotted with sweat, but I couldn't wait to get home and figure them out.

STEVE: *Some of my best days at school were when I went to school at 6:30, did my workout and then got showered and went to the locker for my first class at 8, all pumped up because I had just had a great workout. Even if it wasn't a great workout I felt good, because I knew I had done it.*

I might be thinking, Well, I didn't shoot well going to my left today, I need to work on that after school. A lot of kids today struggle just to go to high school and attend class. That was my motivation to go to class, knowing I had gotten myself up and done a workout.

ED: *I remember treating myself to an ice cream bar at night if I could break a record for my shooting percentage. Or I would go the other way. I'd say, If I don't get it right, I'm doing the whole thing over again. And I would. Some days I would go through the workout three or four times.*

Every now and then another player would say, "I want to do your workout with you." I'd say, "Great, get a ball." And they would go for two or three days maybe, and then quit. And these were good players. A couple of guys lasted for a couple of weeks, but that was rare.

I used to love to watch them die. It might sound silly, but you have to spend your energy doing something. You can be the best drinker among your friends, but that's not doing anything positive for yourself.

When you play in a game, even a high school game where there are a few thousand people there, just hearing people cheer for you when you do something good is a big thrill. That's certainly better than having your buddies cheer for you after you chug a beer.

■■

To be a good basketball player, you have to make a commitment — a commitment to be the best you can be. That doesn't mean you have to become an all-American or a professional. Everyone has his or her own potential, and the challenge is to reach that potential. For some it might be making the high school team, or becoming a starter, or getting a college scholarship. The thrill of competing is trying to achieve your potential.

This book has attempted to provide you with the technical knowledge to improve your skills, but you are the only person who can truly determine how good you can become. You must make the commitment to go out and do it. All players, ultimately, are self-made. Your coach can only make you so good. You are the only one who can determine how good you become. You will have nobody else to blame for your shortcomings.

At some point you must decide whether or not to commit to basketball, or anything else for that matter. Then follow up with hard work and devotion. When you look back on your career, you don't want to wonder how good you could have been if you had really worked at it. Don't worry about becoming a pro or getting a college scholarship. Don't shortchange yourself, but your ultimate goal should be to become as good as you can, whatever that might be.

You must love the game. If you don't, fine. Find something else you love and pursue that. But it is a passion for the game that will see you through. There is no magic to improving your skills. Anyone can provide you with drills and a workout plan. What ultimately will separate you from the rest of the crowd is how hard you work.

Making a commitment includes making sacrifices. You will have to say no to friends occasionally when you have something more important to do. Some of your friendships might suffer. But your true friends will stick with you, and you will not do yourself any harm by having a strong devotion to a sport or other healthy activity.

Actually, if you love your pursuit enough, you won't see your efforts as a sacrifice. You should truly want to do it and feel guilty when you don't. This doesn't mean you have a neurotic approach to basketball and think of nothing else and enjoy no other activities. It simply means you have dedicated yourself to a schedule and follow through with it. You won't spend 12 hours a day with basketball. If you work at the proper level of intensity — which is the highest level — you will be physically unable to work six and seven hours a day. But keep in mind that your hard work will be rewarded with results, and your friends who spent all of their free time "hanging out" will envy you.

If you are unsure of your dedication, make a commitment to try it for a month or so. Follow through and see if you get results. The progress you make should be motivation to keep going. Failure should provide more motivation. If you challenge yourself enough, you will fail. Take pride in the fact you are putting yourself on the line and learn from your failures. Failure is never final, unless you quit.

A lot of people spend a lot of time playing basketball. The key is the level of intensity with which they approach it. Don't ever worry that your hard work will go unrewarded, because the vast majority of players don't work that hard. They might think they do because they play for a couple of hours five days a week, but you can do much more than that.

Your dedication to basketball will carry over to other areas of life as well. The work ethic you develop will stay with you for the rest of your life. You will be more successful in your career, whatever that might be. You will be a better parent and spouse because you know how to make sacrifices. You will learn not to follow the crowd and do whatever the passing fad might be and spend your time constructively. You will be better organized and have your priorities in order. You will have seen the benefits hard work can bring, and be motivated to achieve more in your life than sitting back and watching hour upon hour of television. You will appreciate the benefits of being in good physical condition and taking care of your body.

Unfortunately, there will be some players who do not work as hard as you, but have more success simply because they are more gifted. That's fine. The lessons you learn from your dedication to something you love will make you a winner in the long run of life. The average professional basketball career lasts no more than a few years, and many of those athletes struggle after they enter the "real world."

You'll do fine because of the lessons you have learned. Basketball isn't the end of your life, it's a beginning, and it can help you get off to a great start.

THE FINAL POINT: OUR FAITH

■■■

We believe that all the things discussed in this book can make you a better player and even a better person. However, your ultimate happiness will not come from success on the basketball court, nor from academic success or career achievement. We have both been blessed to score points and dish out assists before thousands, even millions, of approving fans. But our careers eventually faded and the records we set will eventually be broken. The achievements that seemed so important during our playing days are now a distant memory.

So what now brings us inner peace? What is it that gives us a lasting sense of value and significance?

This book would be missing an important teaching point if we did not include a chapter on what really makes our lives complete, gives us the power to attack adversity with confidence and provides everlasting joy and peace regardless of the external influences — our faith in Jesus Christ. We are both Christians, and we consider that a greater honor than anything we have received as players, students and coaches.

Although we both are believers in Jesus and have committed our lives to serving God, we came to our relationships with the Lord in different ways.

■■■

ED: *Determination and hard work are attributes I have always admired. In fact, I have made them the pattern for my life. But while my life was by no means unsuccessful by ordinary standards before I became a Christian, I had to learn that determination and hard work aren't always enough.*

In the fall of 1990, about three months after I was married, I was speaking on the phone with a friend who was the head coach at Spartanburg Methodist Junior College regarding a defense that he uses. For some reason the conversation led to my decision to come down to visit with him.

I really had no business going to see him, because the trip from Indiana to South Carolina was more than a second-year high school coach and teacher could afford. But for some reason I made the flight reservations and requested permission for an excused absence from school.

The next thing I knew I was on my way to Spartanburg, S.C., to see my friend, Scott Rigot.

On the flight I began thinking about my new marriage and the huge change it had made in my life. I am an only child, my mother is an only child and my father has only one older sister. Even in college at Miami of Ohio, excluding my freshman year, I lived in a single room. I wasn't used to having a roommate, let alone a wife. Things were in a very unsettled state at the time.

I was not accustomed to failure. I had always been able to achieve success athletically and academically by working hard, and I thought my work ethic would carry me through any challenge. But now I was struggling. My wife is an awesome individual — talented, attractive, kind and intelligent — but being married was something I just wasn't used to.

On the flight to South Carolina I thought about how this whole marriage thing wasn't nearly as enjoyable as when I was single and living alone. I was working hard, but it was not working. The harder I worked, the worse things got. My wife and I weren't screaming and fighting all the time, but I just wasn't as happy as I had been when I was single. As the plane landed, I made up my mind that I was going to do something about the situation after I returned home.

Scott met me at the airport and we had an enjoyable few days. I learned the defense and how to implement it, but I really could have learned it just as well by reading his material and watching video tape. I really didn't need to have made the trip.

The day before I left I asked Scott a few questions about his faith. I knew he was a Christian because he prayed before he ate and he had also made a few comments while we worked the Five-Star Basketball Camp together that summer in Pittsburgh.

I was not a Christian. My parents are very kind people, educators who hold many Christian ideals, but they were not Christians. I was basically against the whole religion thing as I grew up, because it seemed that whenever I had questions about religion nobody could answer them for me. Actually, I had never really investigated Christianity. I thought being a Christian meant you couldn't have fun, and I was turned off by people who pushed their religious views without tact.

Scott never pushed his views on me; he would mention things now and then, but he never stepped out of bounds. But when I asked him a few of my spiritual questions, his answers made sense. He patiently and quietly explained why Christianity was so wonderful and gave some facts that were hard to dispute.

That night we stayed up late talking about the Lord. I had to get up at 5 a.m. the next morning to catch my flight home, so we cut short our conversation and went to bed. First, though, Scott picked up a small pamphlet from the floor and handed it to me. It explained how to receive Christ. He also gave me the book Peace with God, *by Dr. Billy Graham. He explained that it dealt with a lot of the things we had talked about. "And who knows?" he added. "You might sit next to a pastor on the plane and he might see you reading it and answer some more of your questions." We both laughed and went to bed.*

I didn't go right to sleep. I read the pamphlet several times and did my best to ask for forgiveness, receive Jesus as the Son of God who died on the cross for my sins, and promised to live for Him. I held the bed tightly expecting thunder, lightning or some type of miracle to happen. Nothing happened, so I asked God to give me some kind of sign to show me he had heard me. Nothing exciting took place, and I drifted off to sleep for the a few hours until it was time to awake.

I boarded the plane in Greenville with my Billy Graham book under my arm. It was such an early flight that I just sat in a seat on the aisle, although my ticket was a window seat. I'm not sure I was even in the right row. Anyway, I self-consciously got out my book and tried to read it without letting the few people on the plane see it. I didn't want them to think I was a "Jesus freak." I would read a few lines, look around to see if anyone was watching, then read a few more lines, all while covering the title the best I could.

After a few minutes I noticed a lady walking toward me. She sat down across the aisle from my seat. We both smiled and said hello, and I went back to my reading. As the airplane started to take off she leaned over and asked what I was reading. I hesitantly told her the name of the book and returned to it. A minute later she asked me how I liked it and what it was about. I explained that I had just started it, and as I did I looked over and discovered that she was reading the Bible!

As we talked I finally confessed what had happened the previous night. I even told her what Scott had said about a pastor sitting next to me and noticing the book. I laughed because she looked nothing like any pastor I had ever seen. She also laughed and said, "I am not a pastor, but my husband is an evangelist."

We talked nonstop the rest of the flight. Those questions that didn't get answered in Spartanburg were answered on the plane. She even offered to give me her Bible and suggested some other books I might like.

I was still flying after I got off the plane. From that moment I knew that divorce was not an option for me. I also knew that my formula for success (hard work) was not ultimately a winning one. I had a new formula, and it was not the result of hard work and determination, but a free gift from God by faith alone. I couldn't wait to tell my wife what had happened. She was shocked, but she could see the joy in my eyes.

The experience was just too much to be a mere coincidence. I shouldn't have even gone to South Carolina; the cost was too much and I was too busy. I went to learn a defense I could have learned without making the trip. I was given a book and told I might sit next to a pastor who would notice it. I didn't sit in my correct seat and a beautiful lady sat next to me who wasn't a pastor, but an evangelist's wife. Coincidence? I don't think so. It seems that the prayers of those who had been praying for my acceptance of Christ had paid off.

Ever since I walked off that plane I have been a Christian. I have been baptized and I try to live each day for the Lord. I still believe in hard work, but it is combined with Jesus' formula for ultimate success. My life's goal now is to bring honor and glory to the Lord, and I know He will give me all that is necessary to accomplish this goal.

Yes, I went to learn a defense for my basketball team, but I came back with a game plan for life that will make me a winner — not only now, but for eternity.

■■■

We came upon our acceptance of Christ in different ways, just as we both played the guard position but played it differently. You've just read the beginning of Ed's faith. We hope that you will now read Steve's. Perhaps you can relate to one or the other, just as you can relate to playing either as a point guard or shooting guard.

■■■

STEVE: *I am blessed to have parents who taught me right from wrong and the importance of Jesus Christ at an early age. They made sure I was involved in church and youth groups, but while I was aware of Jesus Christ and His life, I had not made an individual commitment.*

This was similar to my basketball career as a child. Up until my freshman year in high school I was merely playing the game; I didn't understand how to work at it. My spiritual life was the same way. I understood that going to church and believing in Christ was important, but I had not made an individual commitment.

I can't tell you why the commitment happened when it happened. I think it was God's way of telling me I had grown up enough to make a change in my life.

It was evangelistic month at our church, and for two or three Sunday evenings in November we had special services. The first one featured a pastor from another church and was no different than any other service I had attended. But at the second one, on November 11th, our pastor gave the sermon. When he was done, I felt touched by God.

He gave a call to come to the altar. I was 17 years old and was surrounded by my peers, my parents, and their friends. But I felt the Holy Spirit in a unique way. Not only did I respond to our pastor's altar call, I felt called to go to the pastor's podium. I just kind of knocked him out of the way and proclaimed that I had something to say.

The next thing I knew I was telling the congregation, "The Lord has done something with me, and He is working in my heart and moving in a special way, and at 17 years old I feel fortunate to have made the decision to serve Him. I have heard God knocking and I hear Him moving me to something different in my life. I hear and feel Him working a miracle in my life right now at the age of 17, and I am going to do something about it. And I also know that there are a lot of you out there who aren't 17 anymore and the Lord's been knocking on your heart for a long time and you have been blowing Him off. My prayer right now, and I guess the reason I am up here right now, is to say that it is time to stop messing around and come forward and get right with the Lord."

Now I have no idea why I said those things. I also know that it wasn't me speaking — I wouldn't have had the nerve to do all that. But the next thing I knew my mom's friends had come up to the altar and several other people had gone up to the podium and were talking. It was just a very powerful evening.

When you are young it is frightening to speak in front of your friends, because you wonder if they'll laugh at you. But that night it wasn't like that. In fact, two or three of my friends came to the altar and made a decision for the Lord. It was done in a respectful manner and really strengthened our friendships.

So that is how it all started for me — by making an individual commitment. After that evening I learned to work with the Lord on a daily basis.

My next concern was how to keep my faith strong. Like anything, it is easy to lose your fire. You might go to a Christian camp and return home filled with the Holy Spirit, but then you are thrown into the day-to-day world where you are surrounded with sin. Unfortunately, I started to come back down off that high after a couple of weeks. I remember going through one of my daily workouts and hearing the Lord speak to me and saying, "Think how your basketball career has changed since you started working on your individual workout."

So I thought about that and said to myself, "What if I start working spiritually like I am working on basketball? What if every day I use God, whether it is through prayer or reading a spiritual book or witnessing or calling up a friend who can help me spiritually?" I decided that every day I was going to do something to work with Jesus Christ.

That was when I really started to grow. I later became co-president of the Fellowship of Christian Athletes (FCA) with Mike Kovoleski, who went on to play football at Notre Dame, and had a great experience doing that. I continued that role at Indiana University. I remember going to my first FCA meeting at I.U.; there were 10 people there and two of the 10 were my future wife and myself. When we graduated we had 140 members involved on a weekly basis. And the way we grew wasn't by putting up flyers or anything like that, it was by word of mouth and by prayer. It was a powerful group that helped me through many tough times.

My testimony isn't about thunder and lightening and earth-shaking events, it is simply about how my life moved from playing with God to WORKING with God. Before that special evening I had been kind of forced to get up on Sunday morning, put on dress clothes and go to church. Sure, I knew about hymnals and prayer and who I was praying to, but it was a formality — it was a religious thing, not a spiritual thing.

When I accepted Jesus Christ it became a time to quit playing with the Lord and start working with the Lord and using Him in every phase of my life — basketball, my social life, my academics, everything. There were times I didn't involve Him and I backslid. But I also know that if I hadn't had that personal relationship with Jesus I could still be backsliding and be in an awful mess. When you have a strong foundation with Christ, you return to the Lord easily. When you have faith, you see that miracles happen in the 1990s just as they happened 2,000 years ago.

I hate the responses many people give to contemporary problems such as teenage pregnancy, drugs and gang violence: "Oh, it's just the times" or "It's the '90s." That's just an excuse. Things shouldn't be different today than 2,000 years ago. The difference today as opposed to 2,000 years ago is that Jesus was working in more people's lives then and in a more powerful way.

My personal pledge and challenge is to involve Jesus in everything I do. If I have a difficult decision to make, I include Him and seek His counsel. At times I haven't lived up to this commitment. I think back to my individual workouts, which I had performed from my freshman year in high school until I graduated from college. I had made great improvement during those years. I also had made time for God just about every day during that time, and made spiritual improvement as well. I made many new friends and experienced many fantastic things.

After I was drafted by the Dallas Mavericks, things began to change. I took up golf and played almost daily. I had only 90 minutes of practice each morning, and filled most of my afternoons with golf rather than my individual workouts. Naturally, my skills began to decline, so subtly that I didn't even notice. Here I was at the highest level and I no longer showed the commitment that had enabled me to get there.

My spiritual life began to decline as well. I didn't have a daily routine like in college. There I had classes from 8 a.m. to 10 a.m. and then I would meet friends at noon to pray. I might meet another friend before practice for fellowship, and many nights we would have Bible study or FCA meetings.

In Dallas, I suddenly had all kinds of free time and was surrounded by money and luxury. I thought I had arrived and didn't need to do my individual workouts any longer. I thought that since I had achieved my goal of becoming an NBA player it would just happen.

Spiritually, I thought the same thing. I had no financial worries and few major goals in basketball left to achieve. I didn't think I needed God any longer. I never said that out loud, but by the way I was living it was evident. I wasn't behaving immorally, but I wasn't spending time with God and I was not growing as a Christian. Because of that, I was not overly frustrated when my professional basketball career ended. I realized I was at a point in my life where I needed to resume my spiritual development. My marriage with Tanya was good, but I felt a void that had not been there since I made that decision for Jesus at 17 years old.

I accepted the coaching job at Manchester College soon thereafter and got my spiritual life back in order. I resumed spending time with God in prayer and in fellowship with other believers. I realized that you never get to a point where you have "arrived" spiritually or professionally.

■■■

We are so thankful for the blessings we have received in our families. Steve has been blessed with two wonderful boys — Kory and Bryce — and a terrific wife in Tanya. His parents, Sam and Sharon, laid a great foundation for Steve to build his family on. Ed is equally blessed with his daughter Christiana and wife Shawn. He admires his parents Ed and Ina more than they can know and appreciates his extended family, the Five-Star Basketball Camp for its huge impact on his life.

However, the biggest thank you goes to God, and now you have seen how we came to know God. We came to our relationship with the Lord from different directions, but the bottom line is that we made a commitment. It is a commitment that we are both thankful for and believe was the best single thing we ever did or will do. We have shared this faith chapter and the entire book for that matter, because we want to give back the ideas and teaching points that have positively impacted our basketball games and our lives. We certainly do not claim to have all the answers, but we do want to share the good things we've experienced in hope that they can help others.

In this book we have shared our philosophy of basketball, personal stories, individual basketball workouts and specific techniques of the game. We hope that this book will encourage or impact at least one person. We have personally learned a lot from it and have become even closer friends. Our ultimate hope, however, is that this book can make a positive difference in a life.

Wishing you God's blessings.
Ed and Steve